Hebridean
Childhood

Hebridean Childhood

An Autobiography
by
Norah, Lady Fairfax-Lucy

Illustrated by
Mary Clare Foa

The Molendinar Press

First published 1981
by Richard Drew Publishing Ltd.,
The Molendinar Press
20 Park Circus
Glasgow G3 6BE

Printed in Great Britain
by William Collins Sons and Company Limited

ISBN 0 904002 56 X

CONTENTS

1. Early Days
2. The Family
3. Sundays
4. Mornish, Fraicidil and Achnadrish
5. Old Retainers
6. Horses and Ponies
7. Friends and Neighbours
8. Yacht Nellie
9. Visitors and Shooting Tenants
10. Epilogue

One

EARLY DAYS

My family home, Calgary House, was known locally, rather grandly, as 'The Castle'. It looks out to sea on the north-west corner of the Island of Mull, with nothing but the Island of Tiree between it and America. The view varies from an opalistic mill-pond, through greys, blues and greens, to a raging storm – the bay white with spin drift and breakers surging against the machair. With half a mile of white sand and no currents, the bay is an ideal playground for children and safe for bathing.

It was at Calgary House that a certain Colonel Macleod spent his last night in Scotland before emigrating to Canada. He settled where now stands the great city of Calgary, named after our house. The house itself stands on a half circle of flat ground, as if dug out of the hillside which rises steeply, timbered with beech and other trees, to the heather hills behind, lawns on either side with a fuchsia hedge and large rhododendrons to protect the flower beds from the salt-laden south-west winds.

To the west a lawn left rough, which in spring is a mass of double daffodils silhouetted against the blue sea. The other side of the avenue was my favourite place to laze on a summer afternoon and perhaps my affection for this spot relates to some pre-natal remembrance. A friend told me once that she had had tea with my mother sitting very contentedly sewing on this exact spot and next day she heard that a baby girl had been born – me, June 11th, 1895 – so I have lived in six reigns and through three wars.

I can just remember my mother's work-parties during the Boer War, making shirts and other articles, with all the women sitting round the dining-room table while I crawled about underneath it.

When my first boyfriend was wounded, I wanted to send 'pink water' out to him in South Africa – Condys Fluid, the cure-all for childhood's minor cuts and grazes.

I was the youngest of a family of eight, four boys and four girls, and was thus lucky in not having to go for a daily boring walk with a governess. By the time I was old enough, there were brothers and sisters to take me, although I much preferred to be left in the care of Mary 'Suddy', our dear dairy maid, of whom more later.

My first conscious remembrance is of great excitement over my third or fourth birthday. My next sister, Kathleen, four years older, had received a gold chain and little pendant on her birthday a few days earlier. Would I get the same? A table was set with a birthday cake, wreathed with flowers, by the side window of the dining-room, but I had to wait till after prayers to see my presents. I fear the Almighty received very little of my thoughts that morning; but, perhaps unconsciously, later there was thanks, for the longed-for chain and pendant were there and proudly worn for the rest of the day – then kept for Sundays and the few parties there were.

As a child, I was, and perhaps still am, fond of my clothes and the cold days of winter were somewhat made up for by my being allowed to wear a red coat trimmed with grebe (soft grey feathers, almost like real fur) and a hat to match. I was inordinately proud of these.

Then there was the excitement of brothers and older sisters returning home from visits: what would they bring me? Helping to unpack, I tried not to seem as if I expected anything! Now all I can remember is my mother bringing a pair of bronze slippers and matching open-work socks.

Later on I remember the excitement of waking up early on the Sunday morning I was to have my first long stockings, Hossors black wool, knitted by my governess. To my mind they were perfect. I was so proud I did not mind their tickle. Later in life I would rather have suffered cold feet.

Summer was heaven for a little girl. Somehow the wet days now seem to have melted into the background. On fine mornings I would play on the grass, making daisy chains or arrangements with rhododendron flowers, as my mother sat on the lawn and sewed or knitted. Sometimes I would attach myself to Archie, the stolid middle-aged gardener whom I adored,

Calgary House

giving him such confidences as, "I am too hot. I must go in and take off my flannel petticoat". Then I remember clearly the exact spot in a flower bed where forget-me-not was growing and the sudden awareness of colour and the magic of growing flowers. I suppose that was the birth of my passion for gardening over which Archie, and even my father, were very patient.

Lunch, and then the eagerly-awaited 3 o'clock in the afternoon, the time to go down to the shore with full baskets and to bathe. On the way there was a corncrake's nest to be peeped at, by the cart track through the field. I don't believe corncrakes are ever heard on the island now but they are still on Iona.

Then the links had to be crossed, the short grass yellow with buttercups and lots of the little blue and yellow heartsease, now also, alas, almost extinct owing to lack of fencing and sheep grazing. I remember in the *very* early days my bathing dress was simple and I was allowed to wear a string of amber beads – which looked lovely, the colour vying with the blue sea. Later a heavy navy-blue bathing dress, trimmed with white tape and frills at the knees, was substituted. Naturally no mixed bathing was allowed and when we came from playing on the sand on to the grass for tea, shoes had to be put on, although stockings were excused. Mother or elder sisters made the fire and everyone had to help to gather driftwood – no Thermos flasks – and how good the tea was and how quickly the scones and jam disappeared. My mother adored picnics and was adept at making a fire. My father, like many men, was not really fond of picnics, but he always came down to the sand, doing a job of work on the way cutting back weed with a sickle on a long handle. Then the tub cart came to drive my mother, the baskets and tired children home – I hated being sent to bed, and felt with Robert Louis Stevenson the injustice of 'at winter I get up at night and dress by yellow candle light, in summer quite the other way I have to go to bed by day'.

In summer at least there were no spooks lurking on the stairs or in the passages. In winter they were terrifying, dancing on the walls dimly lit by paraffin lamps. From the drawing-room I ran faster and faster until the safety of the schoolroom was reached.

Why do people tell children stories of witches and evil spirits? There was a terrible one that lived behind a big rock above the avenue and when the evenings were getting dark, one wondered how soon one could start running without losing face but still be sure of reaching home safely. Over seventy years later, I would look up at that stone and wonder if he was still there.

There was a rumour that another ghost lived in the room next to the children's bathroom. He was a man with devil's horns and he could even appear from behind the curtain in the front bathroom. Of course as I grew older the old house lost its terrors for me, but it was some time before I accepted that there was no 'man that wasn't there' on the stair.

Two

THE FAMILY

Like many other Scots I can trace my family far back into the mists of time.

We are descended from the Mackenzies of Flowerdale, Gairloch, who were descended from Mary Stewart, daughter of King Robert the Bruce. Because my ancestor was a younger son, he succeeded to the lesser inheritance of the Letterewe estate on Loch Maree. His descendant, my great-grandfather, like many Highland lairds, became impoverished and sold the estate, but my grandfather made money in business and bought Calgary in Mull in the latter half of the nineteenth century.

My great-grandmother was a Munro of Eriboll on the Pentland Firth and a reputed beauty. My mother was a Miss Chalmers of Longcroft, Linlithgow. Her mother died young and later her father, Thomas Chalmers, took his four daughters to stay at Calgary in the early 1870s. On that romantic visit, three of his daughters met their husbands.

My mother married the eldest son of the house, John Hugh Munro Mackenzie, her younger sister Mary married the younger son, Patrick Chalmers Mackenzie and the third sister met her future husband at a dance given for the Fleet at Lagganulva; the fleet being on manoeuvres and based on Loch Na Keal. My father and mother were a devoted couple and, though very good parents, they always seemed to us very much of another generation. Many years later, my sister-in-law made a wonderful statement: 'There is God, then Grannie, and then the rest of us,' which puts it in a nutshell.

My mother, being a grand-niece of the famous preacher Dr Chalmers, was brought up in the austere faith of the Free Church, but after she married she, perhaps gratefully, adopted the Established Church of Scotland, of which my father was an elder.

My father, like many of the sons of Highland gentry, was never at Public School but was educated by a tutor. He was a very good mimic and there had been one very trying tutor whom he never tired of imitating. One day Grandfather had called out in exasperation, 'John, for goodness sake stop imitating that wretched man.' Unfortunately, it was the wretched man himself!

As I became a little older, life broadened out. My brothers, 'the boys', were at school: the eldest, Ian, being at Loretto. The Boer War broke out during his last term there and he wrote home at once asking for permission to join the Army, ending the letter, 'Do say Yes', and my parents duly assented. He joined a militia battalion of the Argyll and Sutherland Highlanders under the command of the then Duke of Montrose and saw about eighteen months' service in South Africa.

My other three brothers were at prep school, Routenburn at Ayr, where they wore scarlet blazers and stockings and were known in Mull as the 'red coat boys'. They would arrive home for the holidays, off the early morning steamer at Oban, after travelling all night.

Of course, it was very exciting and glamorous for us stay-at-home girls. I remember Kathleen, my next sister, shouting, 'They've come,' then rushing downstairs trying bravely not to grin too widely.

My eldest brother, Ian, was a great tease and he would carry me up to bed declaring that he would cut off my hair, of which I was very proud and thought golden. He declared it was 'tow' and only good for cleaning his twelve-bore gun.

Ian saw a great deal of active service, as after his return from the South African war, he got a regular commission in the Second Battalion of the Royal Scots. He was posted to India, where he was first introduced to life under the British Raj, with its round of dances, polo, pig-sticking and shooting. It must have truly seemed in those days that our Empire was one on which the sun would never set.

Later he was seconded to the King's African Rifles and saw active service against the 'Mad Mullah' in Somaliland, with intervals of big-game hunting and other such bloodthirsty entertainments.

One guest night in the Mess, they were discussing the ever-absorbing topic of sport. Amongst the guests there happened to be an Italian, who came out with the unheard-of remark: 'I must confess the only sport I really enjoy is eating.' Let's hope the dinner was up to standard!

Then came the 1914-18 War and I am sure that his life was saved by his being at home on sick leave with a very severe attack of pleurisy at the time of the retreat from Mons. We had a terrible time with him, even in delirium, as he kept on insisting that he had to get up and rejoin his regiment. The doctor had to be telegraphed for – no telephone on the island in those days – before he could be got back to bed and sedated. He came safely through the rest of the war with only a slight wound. He was one of the lucky ones. On active service again in Ireland at the Black & Tan uprising he was awarded the DSO. Then India again and finally he was appointed to Singapore in command of the Malay Volunteers.

Ian ended his days as a Military Knight of Windsor, in a Grace and Favour House by the Henry VIII Gateway of Windsor Castle.

I shall never forget the beauty of the boys' voices from St George's School, singing his favourite hymn, 'He who would valiant be', at his funeral service in St George's Chapel. He had never wavered in the tradition of service to his country into which he had been born.

Jean, my eldest sister, was supposed not to be strong. I think it may be more true to say that she was dominated by my mother. She was put to doing tiresome household tasks like mending, ironing and so on but she was also a fine horse rider. She rode side-saddle, on the off-side owing to an old injury to her right leg, but nevertheless she would often ride in all weather to meet my father returning home from perpetual parochial meetings in Tobermory, thirteen miles off.

My next sister, Tina, was a tremendous character. She only rode when there was something exciting on. Her great love was anything to do with boats or the sea. She used to swim far out into Calgary Bay and I can remember watching with alarm as her head could be seen bobbing in the waves further and further from shore.

In the 1914-18 War she served for a time in the French Red Cross in a

Treshnish Islands

primitive old château at Arch-en-Barois, within ear-shot of the guns, where she contracted severe arthritis which more or less crippled her for the rest of her life. She never complained or gave in to it. She lived to be eighty-one.

Jean was followed in the family batting order by the twins, both tall and handsome with golden hair. Tom the elder, was rather solemn, a very good horseman and commissioned into the 3rd Hussars. Most of his service with the Regiment was in India and he managed several years in the Cavalry entirely on pay, with no allowance from his father. This was no mean achievement in one of the most expensive regiments in the Army. Later he transferred to the 6th King Edward's Horse in the Indian Army, where he managed to play polo still within his income. Unlike Ian, he was not a keen shot, but he was an excellent fisherman.

On one of his leaves home, during the 1914-18 War, Tom and I had wonderful sport on Loch Frisa, on successive days catching over seventy trout to our two rods. These trout were not large, but pink-fleshed and the best of eating, especially if fried on a picnic fire by the lochside: literally out of the loch into the frying pan.

I was still at home then, champing at the bit, as I was considered too young to nurse and any other war service for a girl of our family was taboo.

Later, when I had finally become a VAD, Tom and I were walking down Piccadilly together and he was wearing a most becoming little dark blue, boat-shaped cap piped with red. I noticed that almost everyone who passed turned to have another look. I suppose I did not look too bad in my VAD coat and skirt, plump and fair, but I had to admit that it was Tom who attracted attention – and I was very proud of my escort, even if he was my brother.

Hugh, the younger twin, had a delightful sense of humour and was dedicated to horses and ponies. He also had considerable artistic talent and studied animal painting at Caldrons School of Art in London. Before the War he had great success in the Shires, staying with hunting people and painting their horses. He was quite often mounted, but if not, went out on foot and was known as the 'Flying Scotsman': he could keep up all day at a steady trot. On one occasion, an old mole-catcher gave him a hint, 'That's Leopold de Rothschild on the big chestnut, get in front of him and let him knock you down and he'll give you a sovereign.'

After the Boer War Lord Tullibardine, heir to the Duke of Atholl and later married to the famous 'Red Duchess', came to Argyll to recruit for a second Regiment of Scottish Horse: Hugh was given the Mull and Tiree Troop. I often rode with him to drills, some distance off, and then a man who had no mount would change the saddle and have my pony. On one occasion when she was brought back to me, the young trooper told me in a rather crest-fallen voice, 'I'm afraid Miss Norah's pony put me down.'

Then came Kenneth, my naval brother, the clever one of the family. He did brilliantly in all his exams, specialising in torpedoes. Unfortunately, through an accident, he got bad gun-deafness and was invalided out of the Service – a terrible blow for him. However, at the outbreak of the 1914-18 War, his former Captain (later Admiral) Lowrie telegraphed for him to be on his staff in the defence of the Forth Bridge. In this capacity he worked himself so hard that he had a complete breakdown, narrowly escaping brain fever.

I happened to be staying with an uncle and aunt in Linlithgow but somehow I was got hold of to go and visit him in hospital at South Queensferry. I was horrified to find him very ill indeed, eating nothing and never sleeping, in a barrack of a ward, quite alone: no qualified nurses, only naval orderlies to look after him. I demanded to see the doctor in charge of his case and when he came, I was rather nervous to discover that he was a very senior naval surgeon indeed.

I was very young, and having the courage and ignorance of youth, simply said to him in Kenneth's hearing, 'If my brother stays here, he will die.' The Great Man replied, 'Miss Mackenzie, I would like a word with you alone.' When out of the ward, he simply said, 'I believe you are right and I am going to break all Naval rules. If you can assure me you have the right place to take him to, I will let him out of hospital.' Kenneth told me later that my greeting of the naval surgeon was the first thing that made him want to live.

Next day, my uncle and aunt sent me in their big car to fetch Kenneth to their home, where we gradually nursed him back to reasonable health, but it meant retiral again.

In 1939, Kenneth got an appointment with the Admiralty and having had business experience between the wars, he was very well qualified to act as a Liaison Officer between the Services and munition factories.

Altogether, I believe, he created a record by being invalided out of the Navy four times. It was all very hard for him that, in this war, all the rest of his contemporaries, whom he had always beaten in exams, were able to go on and rise to high rank. Kenneth's great love was the Service.

His grandson, now a Lieutenant RN, having passed out of Dartmouth top of his term, later receiving the Queen's Telescope (awarded for 'leadership' rather than examinations), is carrying on the family tradition. I only wish his grandfather knew. Perhaps he does!

Kathleen, my next sister in age (I was the youngest of eight), tall and very good-looking, was a genius with animals. She kept hens while I kept ducks, and spent a great deal of time with Mary 'Suddy' at the Home Farm, learning to milk, as we all did. Patient Mary and patient cows! Kathleen followed Mary with almost slavish devotion, learning to feed and look after the calves, make butter and all the other dairy skills. She would have liked to have gone to the Dairy School at Kilmarnock, but that was not the 'thing' to do in our day.

After I was widowed, she came to live with me and had her own cows. The Dairy Instructress from the East of Scotland Agricultural College said, 'I wish I could say that I had taught Miss Mackenzie to make butter.' The Agricultural Adviser admitted to her that many of the old ways with cows and calves, learnt from Mary 'Suddy', were better than the modern ones.

We lived a very free life but there were certain unbreakable rules. My father, having been Master of the Whitehaven Harriers, kept his hunting horn in the porch and if we were seen to be too many in the boat, going too far out to sea, or any other unacceptable behaviour, the horn was blown. It was a law of the Medes and the Persians, and home we had to come at once.

The horn was not only a means of saving us from our own follies. It

Ulva Ferry

was also my father's way of rescuing himself from any unforeseen predicament or emergency, like the unexpected arrival of guests or his need for the services of any member of his family. Then the horn would be blown and we would *all* drop whatever we were doing and run to his side from all directions.

Christmas was always a wonderful time at Calgary. In the billiards room there was always the Christmas tree, set up by the faithful Archie, and reaching almost to the roof. Children came from all our own cottages, as well as Treshnish, Ensay and Haunn and had a huge tea round the table in the servants' hall. Then the tree was lit and we all assembled in the billiards room. Mother would give each child a small gift. After that came games. One year a naval friend of Kenneth's suggested a pillow fight. Pandemonium ensued and a wall of grown-ups had to protect the tree! Ever after this the proceedings were always wound up with a pillow fight. Before they left, each child was given an orange and a bag of sweeties from the tree – the oranges hanging by a linen thread through the centre and the sweeties in coloured bags of gauze made by Mother.

In the evening there would be a dance for the tenants. Ensay, on the way to Treshnish, was farmed by John MacDougal. John, who became a Sergeant in the Scottish Horse, was an excellent piper and came to play for us on special occasions like the tenants' dance. The best thing was his playing reels which were the greatest fun, even my mother being 'lifted' for a reel. I never quite mastered the more complicated dances like the 'Circassian Circle' but was guided through them by expert partners. I loved the reels and leapt round the floor in the arms of a stalwart shepherd or lobster fisher for a polka or schottische. Once when Tina's partner in a polka was bitten by her over-protective Cairn terrier, he only said, 'the terrier is very wise.'

These dances were held in the billiards room which my grandfather had built on to the house, but a billiards table was never installed so it was used for everything from a church hall to dances.

I make no apology for including these brief pen pictures on my brothers and sisters. In their various and varied careers after they left the

26

island, they never ceased to be influenced by the part their island upbringing played in their formative years. All of us over the years returned to Mull whenever we could to draw fresh strength from the scenes of our childhood.

SUNDAYS

Both Mother and Father observed Sunday with great reverence. Although to modern eyes it may look like a highly disciplined, even severe day for us children, I look back now on the Sundays of my childhood as happy, even peaceful days.

Sundays started, as did every other day, with family prayers, attended by all members of the indoor staff. Sundays only differed from weekdays in that morning prayers started half an hour later, at 9.00 a.m. instead of 8.30 a.m. After that it was not a matter of who was going to church. It was merely a question of how. Only severe illness was accepted as an excuse for absence.

The main conveyance was the tea cart in which my parents sat side by side in the front seat, whilst my sisters and any guests were crowded in behind. When I was little, I would be stuffed in somewhere. The overflow came along behind in the tub cart. Weather or the state of the roads were no deterrent. When the roads were slippy, frost cages were inserted in the horses' shoes, which meant special shoes being fitted for the winter. This meant a visit from the blacksmith who had his smithy nearby. I would stand for ages watching him at work and one of my great childhood treats was to be allowed to blow the bellows and savour the uniquely pungent smell of the old blacksmith's forge.

Arriving at church would be the Forsyths from Quinish in a smart carriage and pair and another with the Morgans from Glengorm and there would be two pony traps filled with MacNabs from Penmore and parties from Croig and Ardow. Many of the islanders would arrive by bicycle or on foot so that the small church was always full.

As we grew older Hugh, Kathleen and I were allowed to go to church

31

Calgary Bay

on horseback. This was quite splendid because it was the only possible circumstance under which we were allowed to ride on the Lord's Day. Years later when I had to open a sale in aid of a Church of Scotland old peoples' home, I said that I hoped I had been brought up a devout church-goer but that I had to admit that being allowed to ride to and from church as a young girl had added greatly to my pleasure. The secretary of the Home Mission in his vote of thanks said drily that he had heard of many inducements to attend church regularly but never one quite like this!

There are many memories of church-going as a child, which I regret to say have little to do with religious zeal. Easter Sunday was always especially looked forward to, largely, I fear, because from the vantage point of our family pew in the front row of the gallery we had a bird's-eye view of smart visitors like the Morgans parading in their splendid Easter bonnets, bought, it was whispered, in far-off London.

There was the splendid moment too when Jess, our collie, putting her paws on the edge of the pew and seeing a rival down below, barked furiously. She was restrained only with the greatest difficulty from launching herself into space to give battle.

Then there were those occasions when we children had to stuff our handkerchiefs into our mouths to stop ourselves giggling, usually at someone else's misfortune – like the time the collection box was handed up into the gallery at the end of its long pole by a new elder who bungled the operation and was rewarded with a shower of coins on his venerable head.

These random memories stem from the days of the old church at Mornish. In 1904 my father gave the stone for a new church to be built. The architect, MacGregor Chalmers, created a beautiful reconstruction of an old Celtic church with a round tower. Instead of the traditional plain white walls he had a coloured apse at the east end with a dove descending with an olive branch in its beak. Of course it was not to be expected that such spectacular innovations would meet with universal approval: nor were they. Mr Morrison, who for years had led the singing, striking the first note on a tuning fork (for, naturally, there was no organ) took the greatest exception. Declaring that four white walls had been good enough for him and for his father's fathers before him, he walked out in a huff. He only returned to the fold twenty years later after the union with the Free Church in 1928.

In my youth there were many islanders who only had the Gaelic tongue so there was always a service conducted in Gaelic first, to be followed by one in English. As we were required to attend both services it was the custom to bring sandwiches to consume between services and it meant that we did not get home until teatime. But what a tea it was with bannocks and several sorts of home-made jams and even fairy cakes and other delights! Then came Mother's Bible lesson for us children. I can remember Tina, the practical one of the family, listening intently to the story of the lamb that strayed. When Mother had finished her reading, Tina, her brow wrinkled in bewilderment, asked, 'Why did he not put them in a fank?' – a 'fank' being the island word for a sheep pen. She could not understand such evidence of carelessness on the part of the shepherd.

It was always cold supper on Sunday evening which we were required to clear away but it was left to the servants to wash up the following day. After that Mother played three hymns on the piano before evening prayers at 9.30 p.m. which the grooms were expected to attend and so to bed, as Samuel Pepys was wont to remark.

The only variation to this strict Sunday routine was on the Sundays when the morning service was held at the other church in the parish at Kilninian.

On Kilninian Sundays, Father had his own service in the billiards room attended by most of the families from the nearby cottages. However we always made the longer journey to Kilninian church on its Communion Sundays. Then we would drive over the hill by what was known as the Minister's road, a hill track made many years before to enable the minister of the day to take a short cut to his church rather than go by the winding road which followed the coast line.

Kilninian was much the older of the two churches, being pre-Reformation with the long communion table set right down the

Kilninian Church

Kilmore Church

middle of the centre aisle. It was not generally so well attended as Mornish because of its distance from the more populated part of the parish. Indeed I once remember my father preaching to an empty church apart from the family, and being amused to see Punch, our Cairn terrier, sitting bolt upright on the pulpit steps on guard next to Father's booted and spurred legs.

Talking with friends about the old days, they often seemed surprised at our taking the dogs to church. I suppose people do not take their pets to church much nowadays but it never seemed strange to us. In my day Church was for *all* the family.

Particularly on 'Kilninian Sundays' in the summer my father liked to take a walk in the afternoons to look at his mares and their foals grazing. As he grew older the distance became too far for him and he and Mother drove in the tub whilst the rest of us walked. This, in turn, marked a variation in the routine, and Sunday picnics were instituted.

It also marked the beginning of the end of an era.

Four

MORNISH, FRAICIDIL AND ACHNADRISH

Calgary House on the Mornish estate, bought by my grandfather in 1870, was the flagship, as it were, of our family lands.

The estate itself was not large as Highland estates go. In all it extended to about 4,500 acres, bounded on the north and west by the sea and on the landward side by the lands of Torllisk. The shooting was far better in those days than it is today, although it was never as grand as the moors of the Scottish mainland with their armies of beaters and large bags.

The game on Mornish included grouse, black game, hares and rabbits with some deer stalking thrown in, but the most sporting of all were the snipe and woodcock. It made for good rough shooting for the keen sportsman, willing to take plenty of exercise and work for his bag.

My eldest brother, Ian, was the keenest shot in the family and he would never give up even if the chance of just one more shot meant a diversion of a few miles on the way home. I should know, for he usually enlisted my help in beating for him and I think that sometimes I walked a great deal further than he did, making wide detours to get behind the birds and drive them over to him. Often as we headed for home at last with my feet beginning to drag as I tried to keep up with his long stride, he would remember some corner which usually held a woodcock and off we would go at a tangent, my anticipation of a reviving cup of tea becoming suddenly more distant. Of course if he did pick up one more woodcock I would be as pleased as punch, particularly as his sense of fair play insisted that I share it with him for supper!

On the western seaboard there was the notorious Cailleach point where the tide raced and swirled dangerously. Cailleach is the Gaelic for old woman and indeed from certain angles the steep cliff face does look like an old woman's profile. It is not the place for small boats, particularly in wild weather, but in the calmer waters of the bay there are salmon to be caught.

The salmon fishing in Cailleach Bay was held by my father on lease from the Crown and he, in turn, sub-let to islanders. At Cailleach a cottage with an ice-house for preserving the catch and land for the drying of nets was provided for the fishermen who were allowed to pay part of their modest rents in fish. The going rate for salmon in those days was one shilling a pound – not a high price to pay for salmon caught that afternoon, delivered to the house and served for dinner that evening. I am afraid this made us rather fussy about our salmon in later years. Cailleach was the venue for our annual picnic, to which our nearer neighbours were asked. In my grandfather's day I am told the wagonette and pair were taken on a very rough road, complete with butler and the Royal Worcester dinner service. Some of the guests went out in the boat to see the nets lifted while a fish from the morning catch was boiled on a driftwood fire in sea-water with potatoes and green peas, followed by strawberries and cream.

This continued into our day, only that Mother and probably Jean, but minus the butler, went in the tub cart with the supplies – enamel plates and picnic cutlery instead of china and silver! The rest of the party either walked or rode. Otherwise the procedure was the same.

Calgary House was a good sized family home – about twelve bedrooms and four public rooms as well as three good attics, built round three sides of a basement courtyard. The interesting part, compared with the present day less spacious houses, was the large kitchen premises in the basement. They were not dark, as grassy slopes led up to the ground floor level outside. The big kitchen furnishings were usual for the times. There was a large wooden bin with three compartments, each of which could hold a bowl of flour or oatmeal. A space between kitchen and servants' hall held huge cupboards for jams and other preserves as well as the household china. There were storerooms, coal cellar and wine cellar – then a big larder with slate shelves and plenty of room for tubs of brine to pickle bacon and ham when a pig had been killed. There were also two outside larders for game and meat, these being necessary as mutton and lamb were home-killed in addition to the game and venison from the hill. All this did not represent hoarding, but the necessary goods to keep a large isolated household supplied where bought groceries only came by sea once a month. How well I remember the excitement when a whole stem of bananas was expected and the bitter disappointment when it duly arrived with every skin hanging empty. There had been rats on the steamer!

The laundry is worth mentioning as I am sure that nowadays it would qualify as a museum piece. It was beside the burn down by the garden. The wash-house had two very large boilers and a row of wash-tubs complete with their wooden scrubbing boards. No soap powders then of course – carbolic soap and soda were the order of the day.

Next door was more interesting with a stove, the upper part of which was on the slope, with a little shelf on which the irons rested to heat, including a rounded one for doing up hard skirts. Also a very big mangle, which turned out the tablecloths and sheets beautifully providing they were properly and carefully folded before being put through. There was also a goffering iron chiefly used on the frills of my mother's nightdresses, which were the same pattern all her life, and which were purchased from Steinman of Piccadilly. A new laundress who had been in the employ of the Duke of Buccleuch's household was upset by my father not having a clean day shirt and a clean evening shirt *every* day, as His Grace had done!

When I was at work in the south after the 1914-18 War I had two thick linen bags made with a couple of padlocks each and my washing was posted home once a week. All this has gone now.

Boots and shoes used to come on approval from a London shoe company for us children. Only one shoe of a pair was sent and it seemed an eternity till the pair of the chosen one came back, although postal services were wonderful in those days.

It was also a great day when the coal boat arrived. Carts from all the houses came from far and near to load up. At spring tide the boat was beached on the sand and at low tide the carts were backed up to the hold. I recollect that a year's supply came at a time and the Calgary order was

Fraicidil

piled on the grass links. If my brothers were at home they were invited to tea on board by the skipper. I was very envious of this, but it was not a party for little girls.

Before the family moved from West Cumberland to Calgary, my mother went to her butcher in Whitehaven to have a lesson in cutting a carcass into the correct joints. When a deer was shot a white cloth was laid on the servants' hall table and the gamekeeper brought the carcass in and, under Mother's direction, cut it up. Generally there was a joint each for the cottages and these were all labelled.

For the move in 1884 my father hired a fishing smack to take the stock and furniture from Whitehaven to Calgary. The grand piano which my mother insisted on taking proved to be a most intractable passenger and was only landed with the greatest difficulty.

I think to the end of his days Father missed his hunting and racing. (He had been Master of the Whitehaven Harriers later the West Cumberland Foxhounds.) However he soon involved himself with enthusiasm in local activities and the responsibilities of a Highland Laird. In the beginning he rented a house, Cathlaw near Linlithgow, for a few weeks to hunt with the Linlithgow and Stirlingshire Hounds, but as his family increased and school fees had to be paid this had to be given up. His great treat then was to visit his close friend, the distinguished amateur rider C.J. Cunningham at Wooden, Kelso in Roxburghshire, and he enjoyed hunting with the Duke of Buccleuch's Hounds, salmon fishing on the Tweed and, of course, Kelso races.

Charlie Cunningham's career on the turf was so distinguished that I asked his only surviving son, Brigadier J.C. Cunningham, for particulars of it, which I quote. 'My records start from 1871 when my father rode under Jockey Club Rules and from 1872 under National Hunt Rules.

'During his racing career he rode or owned the horses in 2407 races, 1619 under National Hunt Rules and 788 under Jockey Club Rules. He either rode or owned the winners of 745 races and those placed in 1484 races and was unplaced only 923 times.

'In 1873 he won the United Border Hunts Steeplechase at Kelso, repeating this on twenty occasions out of thirty starts. He was also second four times.

'Whilst still at school at Rugby, on 29th March 1881 he rode seven races. He won six and was second in the seventh. A record never since equalled over fences. That day he raced a distance of twenty miles.

'In 1889 he rode "Why Not" in the Grand National and was second, beaten by one length by "Frigate" ridden by Harry Beasley. He rode in the Grand National five times and was fifth after falling and remounting in 1890. "Why Not" won the National when owned by Mr C.H. Fenwick in 1894.

'In 1892 he won the National Breeders Produce Stakes, the richest sprint race of five furlongs in the kingdom with "Tibbieshiels". He had this mare with her foal, "Rodono", painted by Hugh Mackenzie, who had been a pupil of Robert Alexander. The painting is lovely and has all the characteristics of ease and pleasantness which Robert Alexander got into his work. Had Hugh Mackenzie continued to paint he would, without doubt, have become a painter of the highest renown.'

Hugh Mackenzie was, of course, my artist brother.

When my father returned from C.J. Cunningham's funeral he came into the drawing-room saying, 'Charlie is buried in the most beautiful little graveyard above the Tweed.' I little thought that many years later Maxton would become my home and that I should walk past C.J. Cunningham's grave on my way to church each Sunday.

Grandfather bought the house and the adjoining farm of Fraicidil three years after he acquired Mornish. When Father and Mother first went to Mull it was to take over the estate during Grandfather's lifetime and they took up residence in Fraicidil farmhouse until Grandfather's death in 1892. I was the only Calgary baby, all my elder brothers and sisters having been born either in Cumberland or at Fraicidil.

Whereas all the other farms were tenanted my father continued to keep Fraicidil farm in his own hands and, when Calgary was let for the shooting in August and September, we would move back to Fraicidil for the two months.

I loved this. There was the tingling cold water of the burn, running down off the hill, where we would sometimes venture in for an early morning dip. On reflection, perhaps the best part was the knowledge of the hot breakfast waiting for us at the house.

Being higher up the hillside, the view from the house was breathtaking. To the north – the two peaks of the Island of Rhum, Heskival and Hallival, with the Island of Eigg framing the more distant Cuillin of Skye. To the west of Rhum the flat outline of Canna and to the east Muck and Ardnamurchan Point marked in the summer dusk by the sweeping beam of its lighthouse. From the top windows we could also see Heisgeir's flashing light. There was one snag at Fraicidil. It was further from the sea, and after an evening's fishing for cuddy a long pull home.

Life at Fraicidil seemed more leisurely than at Calgary. I can remember spending a whole morning trying to catch my pony, Boisdale, and when I succeeded, thinking how stupid. I only wanted her to ride down to the Post Office at Calgary, less than a mile away.

It was a free and easy existence, like being on holiday – but not all that free and easy. I remember the occasion when the MacNabs of Penmore gave a fancy dress dance and how lovely Kathleen looked as a shepherdess. But I also remember how, on a Saturday night before the dance, we discovered that a young guest we had staying from India could not dance a Scottish reel. Of course this was something that had to be remedied right away and after supper the rest of us put him through his steps. There was not even a piano but my mother had abnormally sharp hearing. The following morning we all received a sharp reprimand because, in our enthusiasm, we had still been shuffling through the steps after midnight. Dancing on the Sabbath, forsooth!

I remember another escapade which earned stern parental disapproval. A friend of Kathleen was staying and we decided that it would be fun to sleep out in a cave not far off up the hillside. We spent the day spreading dry bracken on the ground and smuggling rugs and pillows out of the house as well as an ample supply of provisions.

Having gone innocently to bed, we waited until all was quiet before

47

slipping through the schoolroom window into the moonlit night.

We crept back into the house in good time to tidy up and appear for breakfast, having, as I recollect, scarcely slept a wink. Unfortunately, we were so delighted with ourselves that we could not resist recounting our adventure. It was not at all well received. In spite of the fact that we had made a separate bed for Kenneth in a ruined cottage nearby, we were all made to feel that we had been guilty of some dreadfully immoral behaviour and we remained in dire disgrace for the rest of the day.

Another house on the estate where we used to go to stay sometimes in the summer was the shooting lodge at Achnadrish. Grandfather had also bought the Achnadrish estate which extended to another 4,500 acres, mostly sheep grazing. Apart from the rough shooting the greatest attraction for us children was Loch Frisa and the River Bellart.

The Achnadrish estate straddled the Dervaig–Tobermory road. An old drove road ran down a steep hill to Frisa where we had a boathouse. There were two boats, one for fly-casting only and the other from which it was permitted to troll. I used to catch a lot of trout this way. We would fry them straight out of the water and I remember I used to make a great fuss about seeing that I got my own fish to eat!

For several years Kathleen and I had our joint birthday picnic by the side of Frisa, even if we were staying at Calgary which meant a journey of about ten miles each way. Our parents travelled in state in the tea cart whilst the rest of us rode. Even if it rained we still had our picnic, lighting a huge fire in the boathouse and setting up a long trestle table. In a way this was almost more fun than eating in the open air.

There was one very odd thing about the boathouse at Frisa. At one end there was a three-stall stable. Whenever horses were put in this stable they went quite frantic and when they came out we had the utmost difficulty in yoking them. It was only when we put them to the steep hill up from the lochside that they started to calm down.

It was generally accepted that the stable must have been haunted in some way which even I, who do not really believe in the supernatural, have come to accept for lack of any other explanation.

Achnadrish

When staying at the shooting lodge we would walk to Frisa by the drove road and then cut across some heathery bog to the lochside. Although I was loth to admit it, I found this a terrifying experience. Adders were quite common on Mull and I had a very real fear of being bitten. It was a fear which was not helped by my brother Ian. As we wound our way across the boggy land in single file he would announce cheerfully, 'The first person disturbs the adder, the second one gets stung and the third one kills it.' As Ian invariably led the way with me behind him this did nothing at all to cheer me up.

One of the great joys of Achnadrish was having Mr and Mrs Campbell to look after us. I loved them both equally but for different reasons. Mr Campbell used to delight me by recounting the number of 'serpents' (my dreaded adders) he had killed that year whilst Mrs Campbell would pander to one of my greatest vices, girdle scones, which she made to perfection, saturated in melted butter and then dropped, butter side downwards, into a bowl of caster sugar.

Every year for some time the family went on a camping expedition, going more or less round the island. A spring-cart took the luggage, two bell-tents, personal clothing and bedding (no camp beds), eatables, cooking utensils, etc. Then my mother drove the tub cart with one or two passengers, and there were four riding ponies on which we took turns. I think we trekked about twenty miles a day – it was a slow-moving caravan, but I never remember getting bored.

There were two favourite camping grounds by big burns, Derryguaig Na Gael and Derracuigh, where we bathed and washed before breakfast – very cold. I don't know why we did not fish for brown trout – we could easily have got permission, but were quite often successful guddling. 'For tickled trout are tasty trout and a hungry man must eat,' as H.W. Morven says – and once or twice it was a sea trout. It took some time to pitch camp, the men setting up the tents and tethering the ponies; the girls gathering bracken to soften the beds before the waterproof sheets were laid down, and Mother supervising the food. The ponies were tethered nearby and my brothers, generally Hugh and another, had to keep an eye open as during the night ponies could get badly entangled, or pull out their tethering pegs.

I think the camps were my mother's idea. She must have had a gypsy streak, for though I don't think she ever boiled an egg or made a cup of tea at home, she was adept at making a camp fire, often with damp wood, and cooking an excellent meal. Midges were the great problem – at low tide we would go right out on a reef, chewing a chop bone, but they followed us there and into the tents at night. In spite of it all, we enjoyed the camps tremendously and they enabled us to see more distant friends before the days of motor cars. Probably my father was the most pleased to rejoin the comforts of home, but I think, in a way, he was proud of the expeditions.

Five

OLD RETAINERS

There were never more than four servants indoors. Cook, table-maid, housemaid and 'tweenie'. Agnes, the table-maid, loyalty personified, was part of Calgary for as far back as I can remember, and before, till at last she was persuaded to retire sometime after the 1914-18 War.

Tall and very thin, always the same large white lace cap, her grey-black hair neatly drawn back to a flat bun. She made few comments on life, but when they came they were cryptic, such as in the summer, 'Is there nowhere but the Castle where folks can get a cup of tea?' or 'He's just a poor tea-drinking creature' – the TT successor to our vigorous Minister Mr Munro who had retired, and always enjoyed a 'whisky and gasogene', much easier to produce downstairs than tea.

When leaving the Island one had to catch the mail boat at Tobermory at 8 a.m. which connected with the train to Edinburgh, a matter of thirteen miles in an open carriage. One was called about 4 o'clock by Agnes with a guttering candle, and the cheering words that it was not as wet and windy as when she got up. Then down in the dining-room she had a good fire burning, boiled eggs, tea and toast. If we were going back to school my mother was down in her dressing gown to see us off and we rushed upstairs to kiss our father goodbye in bed. Then the long dreary drive in the dark with as often as not rain trickling down our backs. When we arrived on the boat the crew were always welcoming, wet garments dried, and a lovely hot breakfast put out. Once when going south I asked Hugh Macfarlane, who always took our luggage from the boat to the train, if he would look after a heavy coat for me that I did not want to take south. He replied, 'Miss Mackenzie, supposing the coat was covered with five pound notes from top to bottom they will all be there when you come back.'

Needless to say, the coat was safe on return.

Later when I was going home on leave during the War – we only got a post three times a week – I realised as I got on board that I had not got a paper for my father and asked the Captain if I had time to go and do so. He replied, 'The boat will start when Miss Mackenzie has finished her shopping.' Nice for the other passengers!

To return to Agnes. She had a great deal to cope with, particularly in the holidays. Then the house was full; with assorted uncles, aunts and cousins we would often be a party of twelve or fourteen at the table. No matter the number, it was always laid with a clean cloth and all the silver brightly polished. There was seldom really hot water to wash up with, and kettles had to be carried up to her pantry from the basement kitchen. Yet Agnes never complained unless meals had to be kept for latecomers. She never seemed to have a holiday, and until my elder sisters took on housekeeping, not even an afternoon off. No wonder domestic service became unpopular. Yet a visiting ladies' maid told her mistress that Calgary was a paradise for woman servants on the grounds that each of them seemed to have at least three admirers! I don't think this applied to dear old Agnes.

Certainly the social life 'below stairs' was fairly lively. The Calgary kitchen was the rendezvous for the neighbourhood in the evenings, and quantities of scones and jam and tea must have been consumed. In fact, it took the place of a present day village hall or the pub. No doubt on occasions half-bottles would be produced from hip pockets and passed around, glasses being considered an unnecessary formality. Then someone would strike up on the fiddle or the 'squeeze box' and couples would get to their feet. Fortunately the kitchen was sufficiently far from the drawing-room for the household to be undisturbed.

I scarcely remember Mrs Gerrard, the excellent cook of early days, except that she could always rise to the occasion when a yacht came into the bay, or other unexpected guests arrived. She kept a tin of meringues ready (cream could easily be fetched from the dairy). But she had her weaknesses, one of which was a liking for the bottle. There was no love lost among the islanders between those who 'took a dram' and those for whom it was the devil's brew. Unfortunately for Mrs Gerrard the postman at that time was a rabid teetotaller. He would shake any suspicious parcel and should his suspicions be aroused let it fall on the stone steps 'by mistake'. Not a very gallant thank you for the good breakfast with which he was always provided.

After Mrs Gerrard we had a succession of cooks many of whom rather lacked experience. I remember my mother had taken great trouble over Christmas dinner with a new recruit. She could not have been very quick in the uptake for when the turkey arrived it was accompanied by a rather odd sauce – the brandy butter melted down.

Tweenies, too, came and went. They were often very young girls from the outer isles, many of them brought up in tiny cottages. Few had even seen a staircase. As one of their duties was to take up hot water in the mornings and the schoolroom meals, which meant negotiating three lots of stairs, there were quite a number of smashes. It must have been an ordeal for the poor girls.

Then, of course, there was Miss Jack who was governess to Kathleen and me. Miss Jack liked to appear rather superior to the rest of the staff. This did not go down well, particularly with Angus the boatman. Meeting him one afternoon he said to me, 'It will be a great night for the fishing tonight.' Adding, 'But leave your Miss Jack at home. That's the place for the likes of her.'

When I was ten, I think it was, Miss Jack was sent with Kathleen and me to Edinburgh to the dentist. I had never been off the island before that so had not even seen a train, much less travelled in one. It was very exciting, and each time we went under a bridge I hastily dipped my head! We stayed with Mother's Aunt Bee, Miss Chalmers, who lived in Murrayfield House, a lovely house among trees and its own grounds at the top of Murrayfield Avenue. Miss Jack, anxious that her charges should do her credit, impressed on us how very particular Aunt Bee was. She was in such a fluster when we arrived at the rather grand house that she tipped the cabbie a golden half-sovereign by mistake for 6d – much to her distress!

Aunt Bee was, in fact, very sweet and in her old age given over to 'good works'. As a girl she had run away from home to go on the stage. Hastily retrieved by her parents, she was made to promise *never* to enter a theatre again. This promise she had bravely kept.

Murrayfield House kept open house to all the nephews and nieces and their families who wished a day or two in Edinburgh. During the War, Tina and I stayed there while doing Red Cross work. One evening Aunt Bee gave a dinner party for quite a number of naval officers from the Fleet which was currently in the Forth.

During dinner the conversation turned to the War and I remember vividly one of them saying, 'We feel selfish having our comfortable cabins on board when we think of the men in the trenches up to their knees in mud. On the other hand with us it is all or nothing.' The following week came the Battle of Jutland. Their ship went down – and it was a case of all. It made a deep impression on me. I had enjoyed the evening so much.

It was also during that time that the first Zeppelin raid on Edinburgh took place. I woke in the early hours to hear Tina saying firmly, 'They've come.' We leaned out of the window and saw the horrid sausage go by. On arrival at Leith Hospital where we were working we found a bomb had fallen in the courtyard, but fortunately done no harm.

Outdoors at Calgary there were Allan and Mary Sutherland who lived at the stables. Mary had been my grandfather's cook and married Allan the coachman.

We all loved Mary 'Suddy', the dairymaid. She saved us from many scrapes, such as washing out a pocket in which a rotten egg had been broken. I only remember her being really cross once. Kathleen, Mona, a cousin, and I having found a barrel of tar thought it would be fun to black our faces and arms. Then later we applied to Mary to get it off with fresh butter. We never repeated the exploit! Mary was small and neat with tidy white hair and, when not actually feeding calves or hens, had a spotless white apron to be covered with layers of coarser ones for the dirty jobs. How it was all done I don't know. There was only a cold tap and all the hot water had to be heated in a large boiler which produced the many gallons

Duart Castle

needed for the dairy, mixing hens' food, warm drinks for a calving cow and all the washing in the 'cows' kitchen, which came between the byre and Mary's kitchen. Mary even found time to turn her hand to cooking. There was always a girdle with fresh scones on the open fire. These she would split and spread with fresh butter and strawberry jam.

She had a young girl to help her who slept in a box bed let into the kitchen wall. I always thought this to be great fun but perhaps would have thought differently if I had ever had to try it.

To her many responsibilities Mary added that of Postmistress. The Post Office was in a corner of the kitchen nearest the door. It may seem an odd arrangement nowadays. It came about because the Post Office had asked my grandfather for leave to erect a hut on the shore to shelter instruments connected with the telegraph cable over to Tiree. Grandfather agreed provided they would give him a Post Office in the stable yard. This meant we had the short address of Calgary, Isle of Mull. Once I was reproved for not having written home from school. About six weeks later the letter arrived having been to Calgary in Canada and back, and I was vindicated!

Mary died not very long after the end of the 1914-18 War. I had just finished my horticultural training and was at my first job when I received the news. I wept copious tears.

After Mary's death Allan came down to the house for his main meal. One day the cook burst into the dining-room where we were all at breakfast shouting, 'Miss Tina come at once Allan is dying.' Happily it was a considerable exaggeration. The old man had only fainted, and lived on for quite a few more years.

Angus, tall and dignified and very handsome, with a square red beard turning to grey, had started his career at Calgary with my grandfather. He had charge of the boats, the woods and the sawmill, the latter a circular saw run by a water wheel. He and Calum kept the house supplied with firewood which was brought to the house in a spring cart by Islesmen. They also made all the fencing and gate-posts for the estate. My father got the blacksmith to make a cradle slung over a saddle and this was loaded with the posts which the Islesmen then carried sometimes for miles to those remote parts which were inaccessible to a cart. Before coming to Calgary, Angus had been a professional lobster fisher. He taught us how to bait the creels and where to set them so that eventually we became quite expert.

While I was still at home early in the War, being considered too young to nurse, I served a severe apprenticeship under Angus. Often taking one oar each we would row right out to the mouth of the bay; then I would take both oars and keep the boat steady while he lifted and re-baited the creels. It was a difficult job, particularly if there was a wind which was almost always, the boat having to be in precisely the right spot before he would let the creel down. In stormy weather working near the sharp reefs was quite scary. There were also other dangers such as once when I was in the bow and must have carelessly lifted a crab in the wrong way. It caught my thumb in its powerful claw. In an instant the watchful Angus had sprung to my aid and wrenched the offending claw off. I felt happier after that when I realised that he really had my safety at heart!

All the same it was the long calm summer evenings when I could go out cuddy fishing with Angus that I liked the best. 'Cuddy' is the island name for what are more generally known as saithes. I now no longer remember how many fish we caught but the memory of those gentle evening noises, the distant call of the curlew or the whistling of the oyster-catchers nearby as the setting sun was reflected in the still waters of the bay will remain with me all my life.

Calum, Angus's work mate, was full of Highland charm and had very little English. He came to the house each morning to clean the boots and shoes and do various small jobs in the house. One day he proudly announced, "I have sorted the lavender." (W.C.)! Again when rowing the boat he cried excitedly, "Look, look at the ottoman." – otters were not often seen. Calum was a member of the Mull troop of the Scottish Horse and when stationed in England before going to Gallipoli he was on the Mess staff. My brother Hugh, then a junior captain, had difficulty in persuading Calum not to run to him with the first helpings. After surviving

Ben More

three-quarters of the Gallipoli campaign and two years at the remount Depot at Cantara on the Suez Canal his one comment on the War was, 'It's a terrible country Egypt – my very drawers were full of sand!'

When after the War a Mr Gush bought the wreck of the Union Castle liner which had sunk off Cailleach Point he made his headquarters on Calgary Bay. He soon offended Angus 'I will never trust that man again,' he declared. 'He fished on Sunday' – may that not be the root of some of Scotland's troubles today?

The grooms were also in Gallipoli. Johnnie MacFarlane, who came back, was very Highland, politely never saying 'you' to your face. He would ask me in the morning, 'What pony will Miss Norah be riding this afternoon?' Shortly after I had used all my Post Office savings to buy a light modern side-saddle Johnnie told me, 'I tried Mrs Ian on Miss Norah's saddle but she jutted out all round.' Mrs Ian was Irish, large and stout.

Duncan Cameron was not one of the lucky ones. His grave, marked with a simple cross, looks out over the Dardanelles. A long cry from Calgary Bay. Johnnie Mitchell our gamekeeper's son was also killed in the War. His father never got over the tragedy and died by his own hand.

Archie McNeil, the gardener, was someone special to me, a very solid bachelor of few words. As a teenager I must have been a great trial to him, having read gardening books. I persuaded my parents to get Archie to trench the herbaceous borders on each side of the four central kitchen-garden paths, which I then replanted. Sometimes on a fine October evening I worked on by moonlight, such was my enthusiasm. Mercifully, it was rewarded and the borders flourished. How Archie achieved what he did in his daily round I cannot think. He began by bringing in coal, then wheeling the huge covered barrow with all the rubbish up to the manure heap at the Square, as the stables and home farm were called. There were three lawns to cut with a hand machine, two avenues to keep tidy, many flower beds round the house, as well as the kitchen garden to keep in perfect order. We did help with fruit picking, but a wonderful variety of vegetables arrived at the back door almost all the year round.

The kitchen garden, I suppose about one acre in size, down a steep hill from the house, was a great delight to me. Herbaceous borders edged the four central paths. There was a big fruit cage in one corner and the other three corners were used for rotation crops. My particular pride and joy was the asparagus bed whose crops surpassed in flavour any that I have since eaten, probably due to its annual dressing of seaweed.

On the south facing wall there was a Malmaison Rose, smuggled through the customs from Cannes by Aunt Nellie in her umbrella! It is still flowering, and must be nearly a hundred years old.

Mother had handed over the arranging of the flowers in the house to Tina, and I helped with this. We carried large baskets of flowers up to the house about twice a week but had to be careful not to include anything which would upset our father's asthma. He himself did not seem to take any notice of the flowers, but one evening when the drawing-room had been put back in order after the chimney had been swept and we were taking vases of flowers in, he looked up vaguely and said, 'That's it, I could not think what was wrong with the room.'

In the frustrating days of 1914-1915 I complained to Mother that picking and arranging the flowers took up too much time, but she very firmly said, 'The house must be kept up as usual for those on leave to enjoy.'

Kenneth gave me as a Christmas present a book, *Saturday in my Garden*, from which I learned a lot, especially about taking cuttings. One of my great successes was with a lovely double pink tree-peony. After the War I went to Reading Agricultural College and managed to obtain a Diploma in Horticulture. In the summer holidays we had to do a certain amount of practical work and I was lucky enough to do this at Inverewe, and every day the great Osgood Mackenzie, a distant kinsman, took me on an instructional round of that wonderful peninsula on the west coast of Scotland.

The woods on the south side of the Calgary grounds were a great pleasure to us all. There was a path through them which came out just above the sands. Mother had seats built on this at various points with vistas cut through the trees in which rhododendrons were planted and which gave splendid views of the sea. When the snowdrops had finished flowering, Archie would give us a big bucket of the bulbs and we each had to take a handful and plant them where we liked. After that there were daffodils to be divided and these made a lovely glade. This random planting of the bulbs made each successive spring a delight.

In the spruce trees below the path there was a heronry. Very oddly, the spring before this part of the wood was due to be cut down and the timber sold, the herons migrated to the beech wood on the other side of the bay. How did they know? Every spring they had a 'parliament' on the sands, making a complete circle with one heron in the centre. Did they decide the move then?

Six

HORSES AND PONIES

Horses and ponies have always played a great part in my life. When Father first came to Calgary he found that the progeny of his hunter mares grew to no more than polo pony size so after much thought and investigation, he decided that the best thing to do was to concentrate on the native ponies, the Western Island type of Highland pony. He did, however, have a well-matched pair of chestnuts which drew the wagonette or tea cart to church and back, five miles each way, on Sundays, as well as being used for visiting or meeting guests at Tobermory off the steamer. Allan Sutherland, the stud-groom and coachman, often had quite a long wait for the boat. Having a taste for strong drink it was perhaps inevitable that by the time the guests arrived he would be rather the worse for wear.

I remember one party of rather shaken guests arriving earlier than expected. They had told us that for quite a lot of the way they had come at full gallop, Allan waving his whip and shouting, 'Clear the road, clear the road, the Calgary carriage is coming!' One of the guests eventually got on to the box and secured the reins from Allan. After that Allan was relieved of that particular duty.

Safely at home, however, Allan was a first-class stud-groom. With two under-grooms to assist him, he turned the horses and harness out beautifully. The stable was always immaculate, the straw bedding being finished off in a plait. Clipping, which Allan did himself, must have been very tedious, with hand clippers and then a singeing lamp. Then to be more up to date a standing machine was bought, turned by a handle. We quite often took a spell at this. Allan also looked after the mares and two stallions, 'The Syrian' (Arab) and 'Islesman' (Highland) and in consultation with my father saw to the mating.

River Bellart

In old age 'The Syrian' must have remembered his youth in the East where he would have lived with his owners in their tents. He took to undoing the catch of his box, coming up the avenue and climbing the steps to the front door!

There were several thoroughbred mares, and their offspring by 'Islesman' became very good hunters, Kathleen riding one of these side-saddle with the Atherstone Hounds. Then there were 'Juliet' and 'Daisy', two wonderful children's ponies. 'Juliet', I think, was Welsh, and 'Daisy' was always called Shetland but must have had 'foreign' blood. She was bigger and narrower than a Shetland. 'Daisy' also went in harness, to a little tub cart which we were allowed to drive on our own. Poor 'Daisy', she eventually had to be put to sleep, another pony having kicked her and broken her leg. Many tears.

Kathleen and I had wonderful times riding 'Juliet' and 'Daisy', and there must have been another reliable pony, as our cousin, Mona was often at Calgary and we all went out together – sometimes on the hill sitting backwards and letting the ponies choose the way and sometimes riding in double harness, having the offside pony's near rein on the near pony's offside, and vice versa.

One very hot day as we came home by the sands we thought it would be fun to see what it felt like riding the ponies into the sea until they swam which they did willingly. We were having great fun until we were spied from the house and the fatal horn was blown. We had a good telling off for that which we thought unfair as the ponies were enjoying it as much as we were.

To return to the Highland ponies, the foundation mares as far as I remember were: 'White Polly' – said to be over twenty years old when she came to Calgary; 'Molly' – a little 13.2 mouse dun mare; 'Boisdale' – the Barra pony yearling given to me in 1897 or 1898 and 'Tostary' – another lovely grey mare. 'White Polly' had three grey foals in three succesive years to 'Islesman': 'Gometra' – unbeaten in the show ring – became my father's riding pony. He also did many hundreds of miles in the tea cart along with 'Rhendle', another grey; and then was put to stud: 'Skerryvore', who won

71

the Highland Pony Championship at the Highland and Agricultural show at Inverness in 1909 and many other prizes. He was sold to King Edward VII for the then astonishing price, for a Highland pony, of £100: and 'Heisgeir' – another grey colt who won many prizes and was eventually sold to go out to Perth in Australia.

I do not remember any of 'Molly's progeny but I do remember my father coming into the drawing-room and saying, 'Little 'Molly' carried that twenty-stone stag down from the hill without putting a foot wrong.'

'Gometra's grand-daughter, 'Lunga', was an outstanding performer, winning many jumping prizes and once carrying a light man with the Tring Drag Hounds. He came in delighted that 'Lunga' had led the field over a stiff post-and-rail.

'Boisdale's grandson, 'Talisker', won the Country Life Cup for best mountain and moorland pony under saddle at the National Pony Society Show at the Agricultural Hall, Islington in 1937. 'Gometra' and 'Skerryvore' represented the Highland ponies at, if not the first, one of the very earliest parades of mountain and moorland ponies at Olympia before the 1914-18 War. My father was instrumental in getting the Highland breed included in the National Pony Society Stud Book and wrote the description of the breed in Volume VII.

During the early part of the War when I was champing at the bit to get off to be a VAD, I acted as groom to my father on his many drives to meetings, etc. He taught me to drive a pair. I succeeded in keeping the ponies pulling evenly and in using the brake, but he said I used the whip like a fishing rod! My parents must have driven thousands of miles in the tea cart. They did not have a car until well after the War. Calgary ponies were exported to Australia, South Africa and America and their descendants are spread all over the United Kingdom and Europe.

Treshnish

Seven

FRIENDS AND NEIGHBOURS

It was a happy day for Mull when Sir Fitzroy Maclean achieved his life's ambition and bought back the ancient family stronghold, Duart Castle. He was succeeded by his grandson Sir Charles Maclean, now Lord Maclean of Duart KT, GCVO, KBE, Lord Chamberlain to Her Majesty Queen Elizabeth II and Lord Lieutenant of Argyll, who has brought new lustre to the family honours. In my earliest years Duart was still a ruin. Just the same, it was a great day for all of us at Calgary when there was to be an expedition to the castle. The drive was between thirty and thirty-five miles each way; quite a long journey in pony carts.

In later years, after the Chief had returned, I remember how he would welcome us with true Highland hospitality, at the entrance to the great courtyard. His pride at showing off the progress of the immensely skilled restoration was touching. Perched high on the cliff tops, Duart is surely one of the most historic, impregnable and dramatic of the many Highland castles. The view from the 'sea room' over the Sound of Mull and up Loch Linnhe, is by any standards dramatic. A large telescope stands in the window by means of which passing ships can be identified. From the top ramparts the view extends far out to the Atlantic and on a clear day Ben Nevis, fifty miles to the north, can be seen.

I remember Kathleen and I riding to Duart on a very wet day. We were taken upstairs by Mrs Cordy Simpson, Sir Fitzroy's daughter (now Mrs Bullock Marshall), to repair the ravages of the journey. A note came up from Sir Fitzroy's secretary who was terrified that anything might interfere with the Chief living to be a hundred. The message read, 'Would the Miss Mackenzies please take off their hats, as they might steam and give the Chief a cold.' We were amused when, after luncheon, the Chief sat on the window seat of the sea room, one of us on either side and a hand on each wet knee. Fortunately, no ill effects – and happily Sir Fitzroy did live to celebrate his 100th birthday.

In the banqueting hall, Chips, as he was later known to his friends, the future Lord Maclean, was rushing about. A sprite of a boy with red hair, he finished up sitting on one of the window sills, kicking his heels against the wall, whilst his grandfather showed us inkpots made from the hooves of his chargers which he had ridden at Inkerman and Balaclava, amongst other trophies of the Crimean War. These are now even more poignant to me, as my father-in-law, Sir William Ramsay-Fairfax, had also fought in the Crimea and we also have a case of fascinating trophies. There can be few people alive in the 1980's who can claim to have talked to veterans of the Crimean War which, after all, broke out in 1853.

When Kathleen and I again visited Duart, it was to stay the night. We were somewhat taken aback to discover that we had been given the spare bedroom. Seeing our surprise, Lady Maclean explained that our fellow guest, Lady Harding, had taken one look at the room and exclaimed in horror, 'I can't possibly sleep here alone.' 'As there are two of you,' Lady Maclean added reassuringly, 'I hope you will survive.' I am happy to relate that we were most comfortable, undisturbed by any beasties going bump in the night.

I rather disgraced myself at the end of dinner. Long before we had finished dessert, Sir Fitzroy suddenly gave a long grace of thanks for what we had received. Not being aware of what was happening at the top of the table, I was chattering away happily until cut short by Kathleen making violent signals to me from her seat opposite.

Duart Castle is now open to the public with all the objects of historic and family interest beautifully presented even if the scene of prisoners languishing in the dungeons is almost too realistic for comfort.

Amongst other family friends perhaps the McVeans of Kilfinichen were the closest. Mrs McVean was a distant cousin of my mother and we always called them Aunt Mary and Uncle Colin. Uncle Colin could be taken as the epitome of a Highland Laird. He was an extremely handsome man with a great white beard. Invariably he wore the kilt. Aunt Mary, who had borne nine children, was by contrast, small and wizened. When staying at Calgary she would sit quietly in the drawing-room after dinner clicking her false teeth, which obviously did not fit!

Mother held Uncle Colin in considerable awe. I remember as a lot of us started walking home from a picnic Mother said to me, 'Go and take the kettle from your uncle, it is not seemly for him to carry it.' Of course I did, but having never been a great supporter of the women's liberation movement, I was most indignant. I remember years after the Uncle Colin incident, when I was a very junior VAD getting some experience in a civil hospital, doing the rounds of a ward with Sister and a senior doctor. I hesitated by a door until Sister severely told me to open it. I think I vaguely expected the doctor to do this for me!

To return to the McVeans, they lived in a beautiful Georgian house on the north side of Loch Scridain. We often camped by a lovely burn about a mile off and had many happy times at Kilfinichen. The eldest sister was married to a diplomat in Japan and in the garden at Kilfinichen there were masses of the Japanese *lilium auratum* which did extremely well. Her two sons Hughie and Colin Gubbins were round about my age. Hughie used to come to the camp early having caught trout in the burn 'for Norah's breakfast' – this attention privately rattled me as my affections were fixed on Colin, the younger brother. Colin had a distinguished military career and died only a few years ago at his home in the Outer Hebrides as General Sir Colin McVean Gubbins, KCMG. He had always maintained that as his initials were K.C.M.G. he would become a Knight Commander of the Order of St Michael and St George. But perhaps even he could not forsee that he would also be awarded the DSO and the MC.

Aunt Mary was a good person in every way. I remember her recounting how she had visited an elderly woman living in an isolated cottage and had asked her if she was alone. 'Yes, Miss Mary, just myself and God.' Aunt Mary was delighted with this reply. I think God was always very near and real to her.

Another family with whom we were very close was the MacLaines of

Lochbuie. Lochbuie is a fine Georgian house standing on the head of the Loch on the south-east coast of Mull. Lochbuie, as he was always known (the Highland custom being to call the Laird by the name of his estate) and my father were great rivals in a friendly way. Lochbuie always declared that the sands there were as good as those at Calgary when, in fact, they were grey, almost mud, while Calgary sands were glistening white. It was all part of his one-upmanship.

One evening my parents were dining at Lochbuie (I think we must have been camping near, Lochbuie being over fifty miles from Calgary). When the main course was served, Lochbuie called up the table to my father triumphantly, 'You can't grow potatoes like these at Calgary.' A subdued reply from Mrs MacLaine, 'But dear, these *are* Calgary potatoes!' was met with a withering glare from her husband.

Some years later when I was old enough to go on camping trips, a party of us rode over the hills by a bridle path from Loch Scridain to Lochbuie. My father spent the afternoon upstairs with Lochbuie, who was ill, while Mrs MacLaine entertained the rest of us in the rather bleak drawing-room, enlarging on how rife tuberculosis was in the Highlands. As a child of about twelve, with a vivid imagination, I became convinced that we would all die of the disease in the near future if not sooner.

The afternoon ended on a happier note when the MacLaines' grandson Alastair, aged about eight or nine, was ushered into the room in full Highland dress and danced a sword dance for us, which he did extremely well. Alastair became Brigadier Alastair MacLaine and organised the Tattoo at Edinburgh Festival for many years.

Death must have had a morbid fascination for me as it had for many islanders. For example, there is a legend that when a MacLaine of Lochbuie is dying a horseman gallops up the avenue. I can still recall feeling my scalp creep when Doctor MacDonald, who I would say was the least psychic Highlander I have ever known, told me emphatically, that when driving away from Lochbuie's deathbed he heard a horse, which he did not see, gallop past the car.

To return to tuberculosis. At our camp on the Sound of Mull I was sent

Kilfinichen

to a cottage to fetch some milk. With true Highland hospitality the good wife asked me in for a cup of tea. To my horror there was an old woman, shrunken and hollow-eyed, in bed in the room. I was convinced that she was dying of tuberculosis and that I would become infected. Of course I never breathed a word of this fear, but it haunted me for a long time till I eventually grew out of my phobia.

Captain Watson was a retired Merchant Navy captain. He and his wife lived in a modern villa about a mile from the Calgary side of Dervaig. As children we quite often rode over to tea, a colossal meal. Captain and Mrs Watson loved to have children around which made it all the sadder that they had lost their only child when just five years old. There was a lovely portrait of her in the dining-room. Unfortunately, for some reason, their well-meaning efforts to entertain us often ended in near disaster. I remember when my cousin Mona and I went to tea and Mrs Watson asked us kindly, 'What fancy work are you doing?' for some reason we found this question irresistibly funny. In an attempt to stifle my giggles, I swept my handkerchief out of my pocket and a slice of cake shot across the floor, which I had been quite unable to swallow and had smuggled into my pocket when no one was looking. At this, of course, we both completely disintegrated.

Perhaps it was the sad absence of children around Ardow which made the Watsons and Mrs Watson's sister, Miss Forrest, rather awkward and stiff. When they trotted past us on their way to church, we on our rather rough ponies, they would wave their white kid-gloved hands rather disapprovingly.

During the 1914-18 War Charles MacLean, a notorius poacher, was finally called up to one of the last tribunals. He went to say goodbye to Captain Watson who shook him warmly by the hand saying, 'Goodbye Charles MacLean, I hope I never see you back.' Not perhaps the most tactful send-off to the War. Happily Charles did return. After Captain and Mrs Watson died Miss Forrest lived on alone at Ardow. When Tina went to call on her, she was a bit surprised to find a lot of well-dressed dolls sitting up on the sofa. Miss Forrest explained that they were there to keep her company!

Then there was Miss MacLellan who kept house for her nephew, Johnnie Lothian, who either owned or rented Treshnish, a farm about three miles from Calgary. Johnnie Lothian on his expeditions to Tobermory lifted his elbow pretty strenuously but his clever pony and which ever Saint looks after the inebriated, between them always got him safely home. Quite an achievement, as the last two miles of the journey was a narrow road, in places not more than ten yards from the cliffs with a precipitous drop on to the rocks and sea below.

We loved going to tea with Miss MacLellan. She despised Miss Jack, our governess, and told us, 'I sent a lot of books to Miss Jack – trash the lot of them,' but she loved Calgary and did not like it being let. 'If I pass the Castle and there are strangers in it, I turn my head the other way,' she once told me.

One splendid afternoon, we were given 'a slice off the roast' which was produced from the press (cupboard) in the wall of the sitting-room and were then told the following tale with many tears. She had once two dogs named respectively 'Kitchen Frank' and 'Drawing-room Frank' and a much-loved work horse called 'Lily'.

'When 'Kitchen Frank' died I cried for a week. When 'Drawing-room Frank' died I cried for a month. When "Lily" died I cried for a year, and I have never stopped crying since my poor brother died!' At which point Miss MacLellan did indeed collapse in wracking sobs. What was one to say?

Out at Haunn which is about two miles west of Treshnish, there lived the two MacDougall brothers. They occupied two small cottages and a barn and made a modest living out of lobster fishing. One brother, Malcolm, had thirteen children and the other, Charles, twelve. My brothers liked nothing better than to have a day at Haunn when they were children. At lunch one day Hugh remarked, 'Mother they have a far better plan at Haunn. There is a dish in the middle of the table and all the potato skins go into it then they have them in a stew in the evening.' My father would never allow us to eat potato skins and we had little wooden platters at each place for the skins. The thought of using them again horrified him and he almost banned us from further visits.

The MacDougall children walked barefoot in all weathers the five miles to Mornish School. We would see them crossing the links at breakfast time and back, if the tide was out, across the sands to paddle at tea time. If we were having a picnic they would have scones and jam to help them on their way, although it was almost like catering for a school outing. It was my great ambition to be able to walk as they did barefoot on the road, not macadam as today but rough with some very sharp stones. The soles of their feet must have been like leather.

When they grew up the MacDougall children nearly all left home and did well, most of the girls were going into service as ladies' maids and the like, then considered very good jobs and excellent training for marriage. More than one of the boys joined the police. I remember once when driving to the National Pony Show at the Agricultural Hall in Islington, we stopped to ask the way. The policeman's head came into the car. 'Well, well, it's Miss Norah,' and the traffic was held up for some time while we got up to date with Mull news! One son from each family, both named Alex, remained at home to follow their fathers at the lobster fishing, the old men fishing the Treshnish Islands and the young ones the coast of Mull into Calgary Bay.

Just off the coast on our side of the island lay the Island of Ulva which once had a flourishing population. It was served by a ferry, as every schoolchild who has been made to learn Thomas Campbell's dramatic poem *Lord Ullin's Daughter*, will remember.

A chieftain to the Highlands bound
Cries 'Boatman do not tarry!
And I'll give you a single pound
To row us o'er the ferry.
O, I'm the chief of Ulva's isle
And this Lord Ullin's Daughter.'

During the Highland clearances most of the population of Ulva were

Lochbuie

driven off the island and left their poor possessions on the Mull shore.

In my day, old Mrs Clark owned Ulva. She was a widow with three daughters and a son at home, the youngest daughter Veronica being a great friend of my sister Jean. Once, she, Veronica and her brother Frank came to stay with us, rowing across from Ulva and bicycling the twelve very hilly miles of road to our home. I eagerly looked forward to their arrival, and sat at the drawing-room window watching the road on the south side of the bay. As soon as they appeared I rushed out to meet them. Frank immediately got off his bicycle, put me up on the seat and wheeled me home. During their stay I completely lost my heart to Veronica, who told the most wonderful fairy tales about the fairies who she claimed lived in the icicles in the burn we passed on our walks.

The Clarks kept a pony on Ulva and the trap on the other side of the ferry for expeditions. On these occasions the pony was swum over to Mull behind the ferry boat. This was rather a perilous proceeding for if the boat was rowed too fast, it pulled the pony's head under water.

Two Miss Huttons who were cousins of Beatrix Potter came to stay every year at a farm on the Mull side of the Ulva ferry to bird watch and much to everyone's surprise Frank became engaged to the younger sister. Conveniently, just at the same time of Frank and Caroline's marriage, an uncle died, and left his villa in Oban to Mrs Clark and her daughters. Although they were terribly homesick for Ulva, they never felt very much at home with their sister-in-law. The Miss Clarks were very religious and Veronica in particular knew her bible from end to end. The Hutton girls were by contrast agnostics. Veronica once told her future sister-in-law of a religious sect that had a shrine where Church of England nuns kept perpetual prayer. Caroline's comment – 'Would not a gramophone save a lot of trouble?'

Caroline fortunately had a certain amount of money and was able to put indoor sanitation into the house, and make various improvements on the farm. She was also a very good gardener and made a wonderful long bed of tiger lilies with a dry-stone wall as background. She had a 'lily tea party' each year and it was very well worth attending. She kindly gave me some of the bulbs and on a visit to Calgary told me with pleasure, 'The best of your lilies are *not* as good as the worst of mine,' but we were all very fond of her.

One weekend when Tina and I were staying at Ulva, Caroline asked her son Francis, then eight or nine years old, if he would like to play in the drawing-room or go down to the smoking-room where his father would read to him. Francis replied, 'I would like best of all to pinch Norah's ankles!' Turmoil ensued. When Francis grew up he joined the Argyll and Sutherland Highlanders. He was reported missing in Italy and never heard of again. His widow and grandmother then decided to sell Ulva, which ended an association with the island going back several generations.

Some of our neighbours were very grand like the Allans of Aros who lived in a lovely old house overlooking the south side of Tobermory Bay. Formerly called Drumfin, it was renamed Aros because the first Allan, who founded the shipping line of that name, liked the alliteration of Alexander Allan of Aros. The house looked out over a fresh-water loch, surrounded by trees and covered in wild water-lilies. We had many happy visits to Aros, the daughter Sheila being a contemporary of my sister Tina and both fond of sailing.

On several occasions the Allans gave a dance. I was unfortunately too young to go but at a high tea about 5 o'clock I looked enviously at my parents, sisters and brothers got up in full evening dress before starting on the long drive in the wagonette. The Allans were very grand but strictly teetotal and when it came to driving home after a long evening most carriages only got as far as the bend in the avenue before the horses were halted and flasks were produced!

Mrs Allan was something of a character, with a very distinctive voice. She was much given to discussing her various problems with her guests. I must say they were often of a rather unusual nature. I remember her saying to my sister, 'Now, Tina, I want your advice. I require a new launderer and when I give a dinner party I have to command three to wait at table, the launderer being the third. The problem is this. If I engage an elderly plain woman, I cannot command her to wait at table, but I will not

Glenaros

have trouble with young men in the laundry. On the other hand if I have a young, good-looking girl whom I could command to wait at table I would find when going into the laundry at one door, the young men popping out at the other. Which do you advise?' Tina opted for the pretty girl.

Then there was the problem of a nice housemaid engaged to a suitable young man in the village. The only snag was that he insisted on having his weekly bath on a Sunday, though all quite nicely covered from the neck to the knee! Mrs Allan was a stickler for morals as well as being a determined 'do-gooder'. When sending old copies of such magazines as *Punch* to the village institute she would carefully cut out any pictures she considered might corrupt. All the same I have fond memories of both Mr and Mrs Allan's kindness. I was often sent to Aros for the night, before going back to school, to avoid the long drive in the dark on winter mornings and this served to soften the agony of leaving home.

The MacDonalds of Dervaig were a remarkable family. The father had a small cobbler's shop. His eldest son started what became a very flourishing grocer's shop. We would ride to Dervaig on Saturday to spend our 6d pocket money on sweets there. The second son was the Dervaig–Tobermory postman. This entailed his driving the seven miles to Tobermory in all weathers, leaving about 6 a.m. and not returning till after dark in winter.

Hugh, the third son, was our 'postie'. When I first remember him he walked the five miles to Calgary with the mail, arriving about breakfast-time, had his breakfast and then went up to the harness room and mended harnesses or shoes. He would then come back for his midday meal and collect the letters again at three o'clock before returning to Dervaig. Hugh was ambitious. He soon bought a bicycle, after that a motorbike, then a motorcar and finally he bought the Bellachroy Hotel in Dervaig. He continued his work for the Post Office and also ran the farm at Bellachroy. When he reached retirement age, he was given the Postal Long Service Medal. A success story! He married the children's nurse from Quinish who bore him six sons. Hugh eventually sold the hotel and set up a grocer's shop in Greenlaw in Berwickshire which was very successful.

When they grew up he set up two of his sons in Haddington, two stayed to take over at Greenlaw and two were set up in Kelso.

Harry Scott, a bachelor, had a small estate at Glenaros to the west of Salen on the Sound of Mull. His brother, Sir Basil Scott, was a retired High Court Judge in India and had married late in life. They came to Glenaros every summer and had two delightful little boys. Lady Scott acted as hostess to her brother-in-law. They were both most kind and generous. Lady Scott was a gifted water-colour artist, but having painted chiefly in India she found the wet West Highland landscape difficult. She was kind enough to take me sketching with her one day – and Kathleen and I were delighted that when staying at Glenaros she treated us as entirely grown up.

Kathleen and I used to ride to Glenaros the afternoon before the Agricultural Show. One day it was so wet that we put it off and left home at 6 a.m., arriving very wet for breakfast. This upset Lady Scott who insisted on lending us dry clothes. When changing back into our riding things Kathleen's were still damp so Lady Scott insisted that she should wear her Ladyship's combinations inside her breeches, and Harry Scott gave us brandy in our coffee!

The Mull and Morven Agricultural Show was held in one of Mr Scott's fields. This was a great occasion for the whole island. My father hired a wagonette for the day as the stable staff were busy bringing the ponies to the show. The wagonette was drawn up beside the pony ring and Mother dispensed sandwiches to all and sundry. When judging was over Lady Scott with her gift for hospitality had a tea party for the whole island. Quite an undertaking which is now carried on by her son, David, and his wife.

We sometimes spent a second night at Glenaros, and the next day started a riding tour of the island. Later we became more ambitious and took the ponies over to Oban, spending the night there with friends. On one trip riding south we stayed with Colonel and Mrs Gascoigne at Craignish Castle, arriving in pouring rain, and handing over saddle-bags to a very superior butler. When shown to our rooms I found a mane comb and dandy brush laid on my dressing table! To save space and allow for grooming tools we only took one hair-brush and comb between us. At dinner the son of the house, sitting next to me, asked if we had our maid with us and had she ridden pillion! We took our evening dresses in rucksacks on our backs. We had a lovely weekend there, and on the Saturday sailed out to the Island of Scarba, the men to stalk, the ladies to picnic. I have never seen so much white heather.

'Squire' Cheape of Tiroran and Carsaig, as she was always known, was a Hemmingway of Bentley in Worcestershire, as she never ceased to remind us. At a dinner party her mother gave during a London season a gallant guest remarked, 'Your daughters are looking beautiful tonight,' to which Mrs Hemmingway, being rather deaf, replied, 'They come from Bentley and are stuffed with sage and onions.' Squire was a very good looking woman but rather eccentric in dress. When she and her husband George Cheape were dining with my parents in Linlithgowshire during the hunting season, my mother being short-sighted, thought, 'Oh, I have a man to many.' On closer inspection, however, it turned out to be Squire. In black satin skirt and scarlet coat cut like a man's.

Squire and her husband were married in 1873 and went to Mull on their honeymoon. At that time the railway went no further than Crianlarich where they spent three days hunting on foot with three couples of foxhounds. Squire was obsessed with hunting and hounds. When living in London she even organised a drag-hunt in Hyde Park. Her grandson told me that she hunted up to ten days before his father, Ronald Cheape was born.

She had in Mull a friendly rival stud of Highland ponies and when she came to see the Calgary ponies, it was a good day for the grooms who were tipped as each pony was led out.

Squire and George Cheape had a family of three sons and three daughters, but the family suffered many tragedies. Their second daughter Daisy was drowned in Loch Scridain within view of her home, to be followed by her sister Katie, who was drowned when the *Empress of Ireland* was rammed by a collier and sank in the St Lawrence in May 1914. Hugh the eldest son was drowned when the *Lennox Castle* was torpedoed off Alexandria in 1918 and Leslie was killed in Sinai in 1916 along with Daisy's husband Tommy Hay. Leslie had been a brilliant polo player, playing number 1 in the successful British team against the USA in 1911 and 1912 and as number 2 in 1914.

Ronald, the only surviving son, commanded the 86th Infantry Brigade, which was the first brigade to cross the Hohenzollern Bridge into Cologne in 1918 and his personal Piper, Duncan Lamont played them across to the tune 'The Muckin' o' Geordie's Byre'. Duncan Lamont again saw active service in the Second World War along with Ronald's son Bruce in the 8th Argylls. A very gallant family.

YACHT NELLIE

Bought from Colin McVean on 18th July 1911 for the sum of £5, *Nellie* was a converted east-coast fishing boat, very roomy, and extremely seaworthy which, indeed, she needed to be on our exposed coast. Being registered in the Royal Highland Yacht Club we could fly that burgee on special occasions.

Her arrival at Calgary was heaven-sent for the interest and pleasure which she gave Kenneth at a very sad time in his life. As I have recorded earlier he was miserable at being invalided out of the Navy on account of severe gun-deafness. *Nellie* also gave pleasure to most members of the family and to countless visitors and friends. Personally, I could often not make up my mind whether to sail with Kenneth or ride with Hugh. Nearly always *Nellie* won as she was only available in summer while the ponies were there all the year round.

I came across the log we kept the other day. These are the first few entries.

Log of Yacht Nellie
1911   Crew – Kenneth, Skipper. Tina, Stewardess. Norah, Cabin Boy. Passenger, Barbie.

2nd September
Wind S.W. 5   A few tacks across the bay with small jib and two reefed mainsail then anchored near old buoy and laid moorings – very successful sail.

4th September
Wind N.W. 4

Forenoon – spent rigging bowsprit and generally overhauling.

Afternoon – *Crew:* Skipper, Tina – Stewardess and Cabin Boy.

Passengers – Barbie, Phyl and Ida Shand. Rapid sail to big bank where one passenger succumbed so returned to tea on the shore.

N.W. 2

After tea a gentle quality sail in bay. *Crew* – Kenneth, Norah and Ida promoted as official photographer. *Passengers* – Parents and Jean

9th September
Wind N. 2

First Treshnish Island Trip.
Kenneth, Ian (mate), Tina, Norah, Ida and Angus. Very light wind going and started too late. Wind fell completely when half mile off the Cairn a Burgh and we had to row to get there, the tide having turned and almost defeated us but we just got there, landed and lunched at Cairn Burgh Mhor, then had a try for Fladda but wind too light to beat the tide so turned and got to the moorings in very quick time but were kept cruising round the buoy by amateur photographers.

Monday
11th September
Wind S.W. 1

After lunch Crew – Kenneth, Ian, Tina, and Norah. Passengers – Mother, Barbie, Ida and Edward Meryon. Beat out of the bay against a light head wind with difficulty. Once outside the wind increased, hauling more to the north and we got round Cailleach very

98

Quinish

quickly. Nasty lop there but *Nellie* behaved well. Then on to Langumull and anchored for combined picnic with the Forsyths from Quinish. After tea Kenneth, Ian and Edward took *Nellie* on to Croig, insulted by Quinish boat which had started first, but soon passed it. Left *Nellie* at Croig for night and walked home. This was the first leg of the journey to Oban for the Argyllshire Gathering.

Tuesday
12th September

Kenneth, Ian and Edward left home early and walked to Croig. Not much wind at first so pulled out of harbour, bumping now and then. Slight breeze from N.W. but tide unfavourable. Took punt on board for first time, a perfect fit. Passed Tobermory lighthouse at noon and had a good following wind down the Sound till Craignure at 3 p.m. when it began to fade away. Off Duart the wind was still lighter and we spent an hour going faster through the water but gaining no ground. Mate's language appalling, but to the point. Eventually we gave up and just got out of the tide race and safely in to Duart Bay. Were passed by *S.S. Grenadier* with the rest of the Gathering Party who waved and jeered. Anchored in Duart Bay and walked to Craignure and eventually got put up for the night at the Manse. The house was packed so cramped quarters and little sleep.

Wednesday
13th September

Same crew as yesterday. Raised a passenger, Rob, the Minister's son. Fast sail to Oban in strong N.E. wind. Here, the first attempt to anchor was a failure as anchor failed to bottom. Second effort successful.

Duart

Edward then landed the passenger, who leapt into the surf and ran up the beach and away. A conspicuous man on the beach turned out to be 'Himself' of Calgary.

Games in afternoon and first Ball in evening.

Thursday
14th September   Procured new anchor and cable, a present from the mate. Kenneth took 'our girls' over *H.M.S. Commonwealth* so Ian and Edward went for a short cruise in the afternoon. They had a small argument re Rule of the Road with a motor launch, Ian with his gift of tongues being victorious. Strong N.W. breeze and two reefs in mainsail. Second Ball in evening.

Friday
15th September   Oban–Iona. Kenneth, Ian and Tina did not turn in after second Ball but packed and had breakfast. Got under way about 9 a.m. in light N.E. wind and went down Kerrera Sound. Wind increasing. Once clear of the Sound, wind increased, and we had a beautiful sail across to Mull, nearly holding our own with *H.M.S. Commonwealth* and *New Zealand*.

When passing Loch Spelve breeze began to fall till at 1 p.m. just off Lochbuie it fell calm. Lunch and cider there in flat calm. Soon after 2 p.m. a light breeze came out of Lochbuie Bay. It gradually increased and backed to N.W. when under Carsaig Cliffs. Here we nearly lost the mate who heaved too powerfully on the staysail halyards, they carried away, and a shout of 'man overboard' was raised. However the halyards made a hammock for him between the ship's side and the bowsprit shrouds, and he returned on board quite dry! This smart shortening of sail was a fortunate occurence as heavy squalls began to come from N.W. We fairly raced along till we opened Ardalanish Bay when we had tea. However the meal was interrupted by the arrival of the Torran Rocks. What with squalls, sea, rocks and tide the Skipper had his hands full and the mainsheet required constant attention. The crew joyfully discussed what would happen if we capsized or ran on the rocks. Notices in *Oban Times*, etc! We presently opened Iona Sound and were glad to beat into it as the sea to the south was getting very rough. When in the Sound the Skipper promptly went to sleep at the helm but wakened in time to avoid the Red Buoy. Tide with us so we soon made the village. Mate threw staysail in the ditch while clearing away anchor gear but it was rescued. Anchored in Telegraph Bay about 7 p.m. and wired home 'Safe at last'. The whole stern sheet seemed to be a mess of raspberry jam on clearing up.

Tina got a room in the Old Argyll Hotel, Ian and Kenneth dined out. Had a most entertaining supper but could hardly keep awake to eat. Gathered valuable hints as to what to do when lost in the wilds of Iona.

It will be readily seen from these entries in the log that we were not very skilful but we did have a lot of fun. There were a few more short sails and then *Nellie* was laid up in the boathouse until 1919.

Eating on board was one of the highlights of our sailing days with the emphasis on tea. There were always fresh scones, a whole pot of jam (one or two pounds according to the size of the party) and masses of fresh

Iona Sound

butter, gingerbread and so on.

I remember we girls also affected huge sunhats. How did we keep them on and move about the boat in long skirts? We always had to wear a shirt with collar and tie as Mother was particular about our appearing at dinner with a scarlet V on our chests!

Trips to the Treshnish Islands in the spring and early summer were a botanist's paradise – the outstanding flower being *scilla verna* which made a blue-mauve haze across the whole plateau of Lunga.

This little bulbous plant grows on the islands all along the west coast, but will not live on the mainland. We frequently took turfs with the bulbs embedded, but they never survived.

There is in my mind no comparison between sailing, shall we say with a 'ladies' or even a 'soldiers' breeze, and an expedition in a motor-boat. In the former, completely relaxed, one can enjoy the gentle swish of the water, with sea-birds like guillemot and puffins swimming alongside and graceful terns and gulls circling and diving for any scraps thrown overboard. On a stormier day there is the thrill of straining sheets and halyards, and the buoyancy of the boat rising to the waves – then the sudden peace of arriving safely at a sheltered anchorage.

Nine

VISITORS
AND
SHOOTING TENANTS

In summer there was a succession of Mackenzie aunts and uncles and cousins as well as Mother's sister and our double first cousins Bell, Mona and Harry MacDougal as well as Aunt Izzie, Mother's eldest sister who was widowed with three sons and a daughter.

Aunt Izzie was a very volatile character. Each year on arrival she would wax lyrical about the beauty of Calgary. This would last for about a week before it was, 'I cannot stand this dull hole any longer,' and she would be off to pastures new. She took Jean, my eldest sister, on a trip to South Africa. Crossing the Bay when it was rather stormy she strode up and down proclaiming, 'I don't get sea sick, I am an admiral's widow.' Uncle Jack Merryon had died with the rank of Captain RN but the old lady had given herself promotion to what he might have been if he had lived longer!

Mona Mackenzie was nearest to me in age and we had a lot of fun together. She once came to stay riding a very nice grey pony 'Lady Jane', and leading a Shetland pony 'Spunkie' with all her luggage in panniers. We went to meet her and our ponies must have excited 'Spunkie'. He broke loose, galloping and bucking all round a field and scattering poor Mona's most intimate garments to the four winds. I seldom pass this field even now without recalling the scene vividly in my mind's eye! Bell, Mona's elder sister, was very elegant and superior. I remember her remarking at a picnic, 'Aunt Jeanie (my mother) has such messy children!'

When a party of us went for walks we would have a competition as to who could collect the greatest number of wild flowers, often reaching fifty or more varieties. Of course one of the family had an advantage here as we knew where the more scarce species grew, such as the wintergreens, bog pimpernel, etc. Flowers have always meant a great deal to me. If my faith in

God sometimes wavers, I think of the thousands of species from the majestic forest trees to the tiniest *saginae*, which can surely only have been conceived by a Divine Being.

Of the male cousins, Tom Gillespie stands out, tall and well-built with a smile that reached from ear to ear. He was a first-class oar and rowed in the Leander Eight at the Olympic Games in Sweden. He was very proud of his election to the Leander Club and on arrival at Calgary would drape the marble bust of his great-great uncle the Rev. Dr Thomas Chalmers, which stood in the porch, with his rose pink cap and scarf.

One day walking up from the shore carrying a pail of flounders Tom remarked forcibly, 'I've dug the bait, rowed the boat, lifted the bait and now I'm carrying the fish. Can we please have them fried not boiled for dinner!' My parents were fond of boiled fish.

Tom was killed in France in the early days of the War to be followed not long afterwards by his elder brother Douglas, a brilliant scholar at Oxford and a friend of Rupert Brooke and his set.

I think I must have been a little minx as a child, for apart from all the relations, I can remember very few of the female guests. I do remember, however, a friend of Tina's who came to tea in the school room, invited by Miss Jack, wearing a lovely pink crêpe-de-chine negligee with lace frills, which I thought was lovely – but Miss Jack was shocked and the girl was never asked again.

Then there were the two Miss Jeffersons from Cumberland. They used to have their breakfast in bed. I remember being sent up to their room with a message and was horrified to see one of them fastening herself into what seemed to me a vast and revolting grey corset. I made a hasty retreat and can remember nothing else about them.

The male guests stand out much more clearly. There was Major Morris, a hunting friend of my father who came every winter to shoot. He was always beautifully turned-out and in the evening changed into a white tie and tail-coat. He was always nice to me and I think he must have set too high a standard for my youthful opinion of the male sex.

A brother officer of Ian's was coming to stay and I hid for ages behind the drawing-room curtains on a winter's evening waiting for his arrival, but the boat was late, and I was sent to bed before he arrived. In the morning to my bitter disappointment he turned out to be a rather pale and spotty youth and I completely lost interest!

A much more glamorous figure was Lt-Colonel Malcolm McNeill who came to stay at Calgary. The interesting thing was that though he was a big-game hunter with a worldwide reputation, he declared that some wily old cock-pheasants that were destroying the Brussels sprouts in the garden had given him as much fun and taken as much skill to stalk and kill as any of his big game! He was also a piper of professional standard, which made his visits even more enjoyable. Calum McNeill built up a wonderful big-game museum at Dungrianach in Oban which he left to Lady Farquhar, widow of Sir Arthur Farquhar KCB, CVO. He was in the Argyll and Sutherland Highlanders, winning the DSO and being mentioned in despatches. He died in action commanding a battalion of the Argylls.

Another visitor whose arrival was a matter of excited anticipation for me was that of Lord Arthur Cecil who was met off the boat from the Outer Islands. Again disappointment. He was a plain, rather small man with an untidy beard. However, he was charming and won my heart!

Then two New Zealand men were coming to stay and see, and perhaps buy, ponies. My father teased me for days beforehand, telling me that they would be dressed in skins and feathers. However, when they arrived they were two perfectly ordinary men in conventional grey suits and very good company.

There were the shoots when two or three couples came to stay for a few days. Kathleen, Mona and I were not particularly interested in the shooting though we liked to see the game laid out when the guns came in. The highlight was to sit on the landing and peep downstairs at the couples going in to dinner. Even better was to rush downstairs to get a picking from each course as it came out, and rush upstairs again before we were caught!

I certainly cannot forget Sir Thomas Erskine of Cambo in Fife who was Adjutant to the 2nd Regiment of the Scottish Horse. None of us, except

111

Fraicidil

Hugh, had ever met him before. He arrived about tea-time, and before dinner when fortunately my father and mother had gone upstairs to dress rather early, a desperate Sir Thomas rushed into the drawing-room in his shirt-sleeves with his dinner-jacket in his hand saying, 'Can you girls do anything about this? I have brought a dinner-jacket I have not worn since I left Eton and cannot get into it.' We hastily tore open the side-seams and arm-holes and tacked them up at the furthest possible place. We helped Sir Thomas to put it on gingerly. This made Tina and me late for dinner and rather unpopular. When we got down to the dining-room Sir Thomas was sitting innocently on Mother's right and never let on that he had been the cause of it.

Although not staying the night, Mr Munro of whisky and gasogene renown came very often. I loved this and when sitting in the drawing-room after tea I would climb on to his knee, much to his embarrassment, turning my head all round the room making a 'Mr Munro face'!

I remember less about him in the pulpit, except that one Sunday after announcing a couple's banns of marriage he proclaimed forcibly that the fee for this service was 2/6d which was all too often not paid! When Mr Munro retired, to be followed by 'the poor tea drinking creature', he was taken in and looked after at a farm about three or four miles from Calgary. One day Hugh met the Free Church Minister's rather dotty son who told him almost weeping, 'Our old friend Mr Munro (they were not on speaking terms) has died and I am on the way to his funeral.' Hugh was very surprised that we had not been told and came at once to give my father the sad news. Two ponies were hastily got ready, while they dressed suitably, only to find, when they got to the farm, Mr Munro hale and hearty!

Many interesting people came to Mull. Lord Baden-Powell came for a Boy Scout rally at Aros and my mother was delighted at sitting next to him at tea and having a long interesting talk.

John Buchan (later Lord Tweedsmuir) came with his wife and family to one of my father's huge birthday picnics on the sands and enjoyed eating 'jeelie pieces'. Years later his daughter Alice married my step-son Brian Fairfax-Lucy.

Frances, Lady Warwick, one of the three daughters of the Earl of Rosslyn who had all been Edwardian beauties, also came to Mull. She was still a remarkable-looking old lady and perfectly made up.

My father was captured by her charm and beauty and enjoyed talking to her about hunting in the Shires. I remember her saying, 'When Hugh Lonsdale (the Yellow Earl) lent me a mount I scarcely dared move my big toe, it was so highly trained.' I think she enjoyed seeing the ponies and especially 'The Syrian' as she sent a framed print of a lovely Arabian stallion to my father. Having spent a lifetime in the hunting field and being the talk of society, she became in her old age anti-blood sports and a socialist. It is said that the material for her dress at a fancy dress ball at Warwick Castle in the very early 1900s cost £30 a yard!

Another excitement was when yachts came into the bay, although it was not a popular anchorage, being too exposed and with a sandy bottom which did not hold. There was Mr Klein (who must have been a wealthy businessman) from London. He chartered the *Armide*, a thirty-ton yawl, every year. Mr Klein was introduced to us by the McVeans and came regularly to Calgary and took us out for a day's sailing. I think the first sail with Mr Klein was to Iona. I was very young at the time but was greatly impressed by the Abbey even then when it was still a ruin and, of course, also by the Reilig Odhran, where it is believed that forty-eight Scottish, four Irish and eight Norwegian kings are buried, as well as the chiefs of many Highland Clans. Of course the Abbey is now restored and was presented by the then Duke of Argyll to the Church of Scotland, with the proviso that services of any Christian denomination could be held there. On a fine day, Iona is incredibly beautiful, the sea brilliantly blue and green contrasting with the red granite rocks on the shore. I feel with Dr Johnson; 'The man is little to be envied . . . whose piety would not grow warmer among the ruins of Iona.'

Mr Klein then took Kenneth with him to Skye to visit the MacLeods of MacLeod at Dunvegan. There Kenneth met his future wife, Eila MacLeod – he declares it was love at first sight, but he had a long battle. She wanted to have a musical career.

Molly (now Lady Butler) and her first husband, Augustin Courtauld, came to Mull on their honeymoon in their yacht with a cousin of ours, Jamie Scott, to help as crew. It was a lovely boat but not so big as the *Armide*. They all dined at Calgary and planned the next day to take Tina and me and two of the grandchildren for a day's sailing. Unfortunately it was very rough and the children succumbed, so we returned to the bay and the unselfish Tina landed with them. We set out again and had a wonderful sail, but the skipper decided it was too rough to risk Calgary for anchorage so we ran into Loch Na Keal and spent the night in Inch Kenneth, Augustin Courtauld giving up his bunk to me, and sleeping in the cabin. My father was very anxious saying, 'I knew these young men with long hair (not really by modern standards) could not be trusted!' However I was landed early next morning at Gribun and telegraphed home. Kathleen came to rescue me in her first little car.

Aunt Nellie was once yachting with her friend, Lord Rendal, a widower, and his daughter, anchoring in Tobermory Bay. They got in touch with us. Tina and I drove to Tobermory looking forward to a wonderful day in the 300-ton steam-yacht. But no. Lord Rendal was completely under the thumb of his captain who declared it was too bad a day to go even up sheltered Loch Sunart, so Miss Rendal enlisted us to help with one of her endless good works and we spent the day sewing shirts for factory girls. An otherwise disappointing day was relieved by Aunt Nellie's fund of stories over lunch which caused one of the stewards to laugh so much that the green peas finished up on my knees. We drove home in the rain somewhat deflated.

Achnadrish was the first of our shootings to be let and I can remember the first tenants were a French Count and Countess. They came to tea at Calgary and Monsieur le Comte came into the drawing-room, bowed low and presented my mother with a magnificent game pie. As we were seeing them off we were horrified to find the foxhound puppies from the Linlithgow and Stirlingshire hounds, which we were walking, racing round the gravel with the Countess' silk parasol in ribbons! It was, however, the Count and Countess who had the last laugh. When the great

115

pie was served at dinner that night it was found to contain what were undoubtedly blackbirds and thrushes with the odd sparrow thrown in for good measure!

Then there were Colonel Dyson Lawrie, a widower and his daughter. They came to Achnadrish on several successive years and Miss D.L. became quite a close friend of Jean – who often stayed with them at Achnadrish, but while fishing she did not enjoy landing for a couple of hours at lunch-time to play bridge. Colonel D.L. remarried and had a son who became Sir Percy Lawrie, Chief of the London Mounted Police.

Then came the Gore Langtons about whom I remember very little, except that there were three nice sons who used to come over to supper and cuddy-fish. Of course I was too young, and was furious at being sent to bed.

After the Langtons there were the Blewitts with whom we became real friends. Mrs Blewitt was delightful, but very vague. I remember her enthusiastically taking photographs at the Salen Show with the camera pointing to her ample bosom! One year they rented Erray at Tobermory. Four of us had sailed round to Tobermory in *Nellie* for the regatta the next day and Kenneth and Kathleen were staying with the Allans at Aros. Tina and I stayed in digs in Tobermory and dined with the Blewitts. We had a most amusing evening. In the middle of dinner a grandson suddenly remarked, 'Grannie, your wig is coming off.' It had fascinated me for some time. Mrs Blewitt calmly said, 'So it is,' and shoved it back more or less into position. We asked Guy and Helen, the two Blewitt children, to join us in *Nellie* next day to watch the regatta and were a little taken aback when Guy arrived in complete yachting rig, white trousers and shoes, blazer and yachting cap, as if going to Cowes. But they both seemed to enjoy the day very much.

Later we started to let the shooting at Calgary. The first lot I don't remember much about, except that we played uproarious games with them. We were not so amused when dining with them to see wet bathing-dresses being dried on the lion's head in the hall and our host tapping the ash from his cigar on to the drawing-room carpet. Mother did

Calgary Bay

not even allow smoking in her drawing-room. When we asked them back to dine at Fraicidil, we were told that they were bringing with them, 'a very tiresome guest who would not eat venison'. There was a good cook at Fraicidil at that time and some well-hung venison. Mother had that brought in and supervised a good steak being cut, giving orders for it to be cooked as like fillet of beef as possible. At dinner the lady asked, 'Mrs Mackenzie where do you get this delicious beef?' Giggles from the family, but the tactful reply 'We kill our own' avoided what could have been an embarrassing moment.

The Innes family were the tenants who became real friends. Mrs Innes was a widow with three daughters and two sons. The oldest daughter was rather mannish, and a keen shot; the middle one Phyllis, was a good horsewoman. Hugh took her out riding a lot and she joined our party for the Oban Gathering. Whether she enjoyed it as much as Hugh did, I do not know but I do remember one day at lunch my father asked her where they had been, and her reply was 'up and down precipices'. The Inneses gave a dance at Calgary which I much enjoyed, dancing a lot with a charming lieutenant RN and afterwards was teased unmercifully by the family.

In the spring of 1914 I was staying for three months with Aunt Izzie in her Kensington flat, to attend the London School of Art where I greatly enjoyed being taught by the son of the artist Orchardson who was most encouraging to me. During this time the Inneses asked me to join their party for a dance, I think in April, if I could produce a partner. Fortunately George McVean from Mull was in London and came with me. I was terrified on going into dinner in the smart house in Dudley Square to find myself placed in the seat of honour on my host's right. We islanders did not know much about the social graces of Londoners. I got through, helping myself first to most courses quite well, but was nearly stumped by a very stiff iced pudding. When we arrived at the dance they were excellent hosts introducing me and my programme was soon filled. I enjoyed it all tremendously, but I am sure was very 'raw' and awkward, cutting a certain Viscount without a word when George came to claim me for the supper dance. I hope he realised it was shyness and not rudeness. Towards the end of the evening conversation was rather sticky. In desperation my partner asked if I had come up to London to do the season. I quickly replied, 'Heaven's no, I am going home in a fortnight.' But I can't have behaved too badly as the Inneses report home was good!

Of course it all had to end some time. The war clouds were gathering and that golden summer of 1914 was the last of an era and way of life. When we got home from church on Sunday 2nd August there was a telegram from Ivor Campbell, cousin to the then Duke of Argyll, asking if we could put him up for the night, which of course we did. He sailed into the bay from Tiree just before supper. That evening he told us he was on his way to Paris on important business and that Germany had invaded Belgium and France had declared war on Germany. Ivor had all the Argyll charm and in spite of the serious news we spent a very pleasant evening. He left to catch the early boat and we never saw him again. He was killed in the Middle East.

On Tuesday 4th August, Britain declared war on Germany and we were in it up to the hilt. The Scottish Horse was mobilised so Hugh and his Mull men were off. My father was created Head Coastwatcher for Mull. Mother formed her work party and before long was off to France with them to nurse under the French Red Cross. Kathleen was finishing her physiotherapy training in London and I was left champing at the bit!

I think it must have been before I was allowed to leave home to nurse that just after prayers Agnes came into the dining-room to say, 'Alex MacDougall wishes a word with you, Sir.' I heard Alex say, 'There is a big liner ashore on Cailleach Point.' After some talk my father returned and said to me, 'Finish your breakfast and go up to the stables and take my mare . . . you will be quicker than me. Go to Cailleach and find out if there is any life on board the ship.'

I have never gone through the hill so quickly. 'Eriska', grand-daughter of 'White Polly', galloping most of the way. By good luck I struck the exact spot at the top of the cliffs where the liner was lying on her side on the rocks below, waves breaking over her deck and flotsam and jetsam being

Iona Abbey

swept overboard. I stayed and watched for a long while, but there was no sign of life. She was a mystery ship for some time, and it then transpired that she was a Union Castle liner that had been torpedoed in the Atlantic, broken loose when being towed, and abandoned – needless to say the shepherds did very little work for some time. In fact, most cottages still have some souvenirs. For me it was my first taste of the realities of war.

Epilogue

Were they the good old days, or the bad? In reading over the manuscript, it appears as if we had lived only for pleasure. Of course we did, but I think we were also always aware that our good luck in belonging to a close family circle with our comfortable home and material security also carried with it responsibilities. I think too there is something special about being brought up on an island. There was a very good relationship between employer and employee.

Admittedly, wages were small and the cottages primitive, but they were well-built with thick stone walls. Each house was supplied with oatmeal, flour and coal. Peats could be cut and wood gathered. The shepherds and the gamekeeper had grazing for a cow and a field to make hay for winter keep. Those families who had not a cow were supplied with milk. The children led a very free life. Most of them as they grew up got employment on the mainland but always came home for holidays. In illness anything required was sent from the big house, nourishing soups and so on and, of course, the patient was visited regularly.

Our own upbringing was fairly strict with a strong emphasis on religion but we were happy.

In the quiet of the night I think of Mull,
And the days now far away —
Remember the children who played on the shore,
And galloped their ponies across the moor,
And a home that was loving, and warm, and secure
In the house above Calgary Bay.

(These were the last words that Lady Fairfax-Lucy wrote.)

Lady Fairfax-Lucy